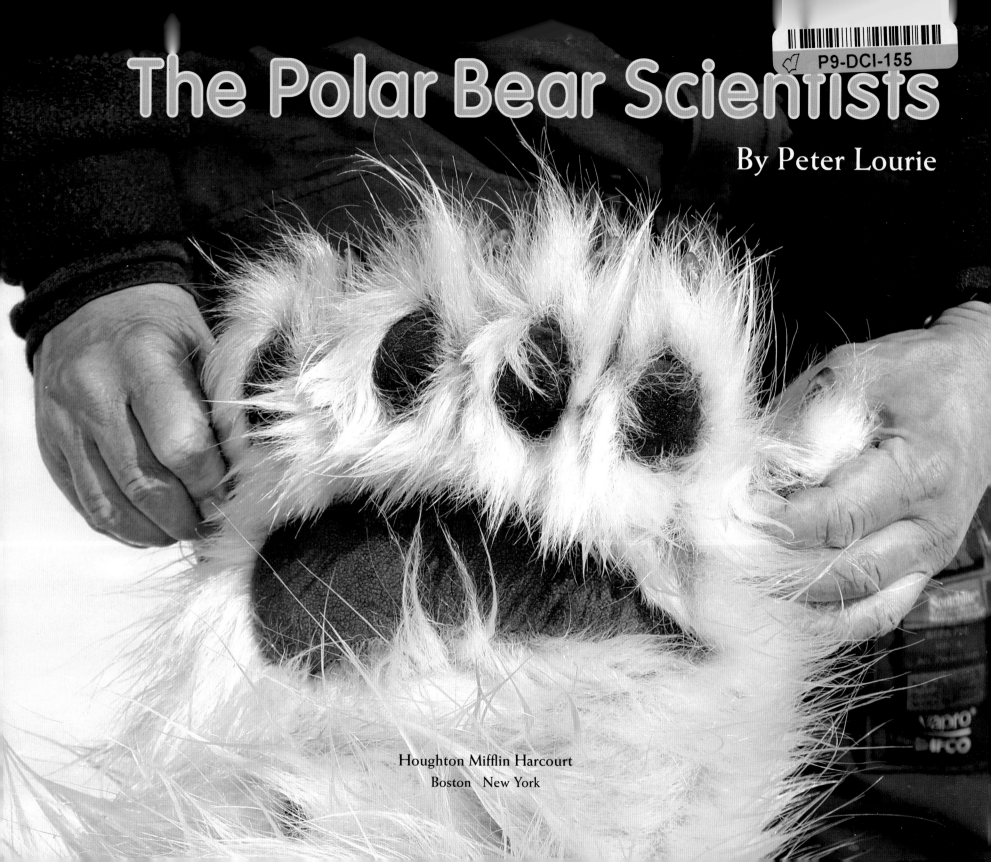

The Polar Bear Scientists

By Peter Lourie

Houghton Mifflin Harcourt
Boston   New York

To Mike Lockhart, amazing photographer and field biologist, and to all the folks dedicated to polar bear science.

ACKNOWLEDGMENTS

Special thanks to the U.S. Geological Survey, Alaska Science Center, the National Science Foundation, Polar Bears International, North Slope Borough Department of Wildlife Management, University of Wyoming, Western EcoSystems Technology, Inc., and Steven C. Armstrup, George Durner, Kristin Simac, Mike Lockhart, Robert Buchanan, Geoff Wolf, Karyn Rode, Craig George, Eugene Brower, Geoff Carroll, Lily Peacock, Ryan MacDonald, Trent McDonald, Joe Fieldman, Gaylen Jensen, Glenn Sheehan, and Ann Jensen.

Text copyright © 2012 by Peter Lourie

www.hmhco.com

The text of this book is set in Weiss and VAG Rounded.
Photo and illustration credits appear on page 79.

Library of Congress Cataloging-in-Publication Control Number 2011003449

ISBN: 978-0-547-28305-0 hardcover
ISBN: 978-0-544-33906-4 paperback

Manufactured in China
SCP 10 9 8 7 6 5 4 3 2 1

4500499892

Contents

The helicopter capture crew moves in to dart an adult female who has two young cubs with her. Typically, the young bears will remain with the female after she is darted, but sometimes they run off and have to be rounded up, hand captured by the crew, and returned to their mom.

The Polar Bear Research Project

When AStar helicopter N73LF lands on the sea ice, the mechanic Gaylen Jensen keeps an eye on how long it remains in one place. Anything more than a few hours, and he starts to get a little worried.

Gaylen sits in front of a computer screen at the old Naval Arctic Research Lab in Barrow, Alaska, the northernmost city in the United States. He is fifty miles away from where two polar bear biologists from the United States Geological Survey (USGS) are processing a bear that they have just captured for research. His job today is to monitor on his computer screen the stationary black icon with the number N73LF. He's actually "seeing" the helicopter in real time on a special website called Automatic Flight Following, or AFF, a web-based satellite system that allows the viewer to observe the travel path and position of specially equipped aircraft on a computer map—in this case of the Arctic Ocean north of the Alaska coast. The flight follower can view real-time information on the location, speed, altitude, and flight history of the scientists' helicopter, the AStar N73LF.

A drugged young male bear is not quite ready to give up. Although unable to stand, he is not yet under the effects of the drug enough for biologists to begin their processing work.

The mechanic Gaylen Jensen follows the polar bear scientists on his computer.

Gaylen knows it usually takes an hour to an hour and a half to "capture" and process a bear, and longer if the field biologists find a family group. He notes that speed and altitude numbers have dropped to 0. This means that the pilot, Joe Fieldman, has landed his helicopter next to a sedated bear and is now helping the biologists with their work.

Capturing polar bears for research is not the same as netting and transporting them to a lab for study. Polar bear capture is about locating a wild bear out on sea ice, sedating it with a drug-filled dart fired from a gun, taking body measurements and weight, collecting biological samples, tagging, and sometimes applying satellite-radio collars or other

radio tags—all before the bear wakes up in a few hours and goes about his or her incredible life in this Arctic habitat. In the southern Beaufort Sea, scientists have been studying bears since the late 1960s in order to gain knowledge about polar bear population status, distribution, and movements. They have collected a lot of data. During the spring

A female, or sow, polar bear and her two recently born cubs. Females may den and give birth on land, sometimes many miles from shore, but as soon as the cubs get old enough to follow their mom, the female takes them far out on the pack ice in search of seals. The female relies on her fat reserves and can go for several months without food during her denning and birthing period.

months, late March to early May, the bears concentrate on the sea ice just off the coast over the food-rich continental shelf, where the ice is thick enough for helicopters to land. Sunlight is increasing by ten minutes each day, so that by May there will be twenty-four hours of daylight. The weather is usually clear and stable, although temperatures can fall to –30° Fahrenheit (–34° Celsius). This is the ideal time for polar bear capture.

Scientists think there may be between 20,000 and 25,000 polar bears in the whole Arctic, with 1,500 of these in the southern Beaufort Sea area. The Beaufort

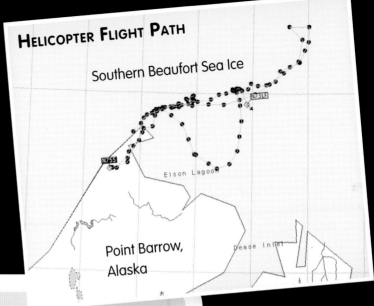

HELICOPTER FLIGHT PATH

Southern Beaufort Sea Ice

Point Barrow, Alaska

The USGS polar bear biologists George Durner and Kristin Simac at the start of processing a newly captured male.

The polar bear capture helicopter is equipped with an "automated flight following" transmitter that allows Gaylen and others monitoring by computer to follow the exact flight path, altitude, and speed of the helicopter during its daily flights—an extremely important safety feature for the capture crew in the event of unforeseen mechanical problems far out on the ice. Each dot represents a precise location and time of helicopter travel.

population is one of nineteen polar bear subpopulations over the entire Arctic. Only one subpopulation is thought to be increasing in number. Three are considered stable, and eight are declining. For the remaining seven, scientists just don't have enough information to determine their conservation status, in large part because of the huge logistical and cost challenges of studying polar bears in such remote reaches. The subpopulations that are declining are thought to be doing so because of loss of sea ice during the last four decades. Changes in seasonal duration and distribution of sea ice can affect the survival and reproduction of polar bears.

For thousands of years polar bears have been important to the spiritual, cultural, and subsistence life of Native people living in the Arctic. Hunting polar bears is still important in Native culture. Some populations, including those in Alaska, were overhunted by sport hunters between the 1940s and the 1960s. Polar bear numbers in some parts of the Arctic have rebounded thanks to harvest quotas and harvest moratoriums taking effect, but global warming is now the most significant threat to bears, because the melting of their sea ice habitat means that they might not be able to find the food they need. The International Union for Conservation of Nature, or IUCN, says that if climatic trends continue, polar bears may disappear completely from most of their range within a hundred years.

The bounds defined by the USGS of the three polar bear subpopulations that occur in Alaska. Population ranges (both core and overall) were estimated by satellite-radio telemetry. There is a lot of overlap among the three populations. Source: Amstrup et al. 2004.

POLAR BEAR SUBPOPULATIONS THAT OCCUR IN ALASKA

N

Beaufort
Sea

Barrow

Deadhorse

Russia

Chukchi
Sea

Alaska

Canada

Bering
Sea

Nothern Beaufort Sea subpopulation
--- core population range
— overall population range
Southern Beaufort Sea subpopulation
- - - core population range
— overall population range
Chukchi Sea subpopulation
--- core population range
— overall population range

Because of warm weather, strong winds, and other factors, sea ice sometimes breaks up into small pieces that may be big enough for bears to stand on but are not big enough for scientists to safely capture bears.

In 2008 the United States Department of the Interior listed the polar bear as a threatened species under the Endangered Species Act. The USGS collaborated with scientists from Canada, Norway, Denmark (Greenland), and Russia in order to put together the information that was needed for the Department of the Interior to make its decision.

These magnificent creatures, top predators in the food chain, are exquisitely adapted to the Arctic marine environment. In fact, the scientific name of the polar bear, *Usus maritimus*, essentially means "the sea bear." For food, they depend primarily on ringed seals (*Phoca hispida*) and bearded seals (*Erignathus barbatus*), which also make their home on Arctic sea ice. Scientists now fear that if the world climate continues to change and if the earth's atmosphere keeps on warming, the sea ice that polar bears need in order to capture seals may disappear and the seals themselves might vanish because they too depend on sea ice for their survival. Scientific evidence suggests that polar bears receive very little nutrition from land, and so they might not be able to adapt to long periods of time on land.

A female bear (right) and her yearling cub run from the capture helicopter.

A bearded seal mom and recently born pup. Bearded seals are the largest of the Arctic "ice seals" (seals that spend almost their entire lives on or below the Arctic pack ice). These pups grow quickly owing to the extremely rich milk of their mother.

The pilot Joe Fieldman and mechanic Gaylen Jensen have been contracted by the USGS for this year's spring capture season. Two days earlier, Joe and Gaylen had flown the five-seater AStar B2 from Fairbanks over the Brooks Range and along the coastal tundra to the Iñupiaq Eskimo village of Barrow. They cruised at 120 miles per hour with an amazing view of Alaska's terrain and landed 320 miles north of the Arctic Circle. Their helicopter flew over seemingly endless miles of the snow-covered and swampy coniferous forest of Alaska's interior. Crossing high above frozen rivers, they saw the path of the snow machine traffic between remote river villages. Their route took them through the chaotic mountains of the Brooks Range, the northernmost mountains in

North America. Finally, they crossed hundreds of miles of the flat, white, and seemingly lifeless Arctic coastal plain tundra and arrived at Barrow.

The pair then hopped into an old pickup truck and drove a few miles north on one of the unpaved Barrow roads that are unconnected to the rest of Alaska—or to anywhere—to meet the USGS polar bear field biologists Kristin Simac and Mike Lockhart at the Naval Arctic Research Lab, also known as NARL.

NARL is a largely abandoned facility, with rusting equipment left over from navy days when the U.S. government, afraid of being attacked by the Soviets, conducted cold-weather research here. Scientists from all over the world now come to NARL to study all things Arctic—the air, the wildlife, the tundra,

A female (bottom) with her two yearling cubs swimming in shallow beach water warily watches the capture helicopter. During summer/fall capture periods, there is no pack ice along the northern coast of Alaska, and polar bears have to try to find food on land and beach areas.

A female (right) with two yearlings emerges from the ocean and onto the beach of a small barrier island.

the ice, and much more. And it is here at NARL that the USGS Polar Bear Research Project's southern Beaufort Sea operation has set up for two weeks at the end of March.

The project, directed for thirty years by the veteran U.S. Geological Survey polar bear scientist Dr. Steven Amstrup, conducts ongoing studies on polar bear populations and their habitat in the southern Beaufort Sea. Now under the leadership of George Durner, the project has collected four decades of detailed and valuable data about how polar bears are responding to sea ice changes in the Arctic. This has provided a concrete foundation of information to help raise public awareness and to help policy agencies make informed decisions for polar bear conservation. Durner now runs the research project operations from his USGS office on the Alaska Pacific University campus in Anchorage, 725 miles south of Barrow.

Every spring, scientists go out for six to eight weeks to capture bears on the southern Beaufort Sea. Some years they have had to quit sooner because there hasn't been a stable ice platform on which to safely conduct their capture work. The USGS formally ran an autumn field season prior to 2001, but the increasingly later freeze of the past decade (combined with quickly decreasing autumn daylight) made autumn captures unsafe.

A typical southern Beaufort spring capture season is conducted out of three locations, two weeks in each: Barter Island (the Iñupiaq Eskimo village of Kaktovik); Prudhoe Bay, also called Deadhorse; and Barrow. To ensure that

USGS research findings are representative of the subpopulations of southern Beaufort polar bears, it is important to distribute the capture effort equally over as much of the area as possible, both in amount of time and area covered.

❋ ❋ ❋

Dr. George Durner holds up a polar bear paw to display its size. Dr. Durner recently assumed responsibility as the Polar Bear Research Project leader. Dr. Steve Amstrup served in that position for more than thirty years.

Mike Lockhart and Kristin Simac hold an anesthetized cub before processing begins.

A size-ten boot print next to the rear print of a young male polar bear.

A Conversation with Dr. Steven Amstrup About Polar Bear Research

In the whole world, there are probably fewer than thirty people who spend all or most of their job working with polar bears. A veteran polar bear biologist, and the godfather of Alaskan polar bear research for the past thirty years, Dr. Steven Amstrup has worked full-time on polar bears since he joined the Polar Bear Research Project in 1980.

Steve loves these animals because they're the largest bears in the world and they live in the most mysterious environment. "Plus," he says, "polar bears are the apex predator. If polar bears are doing well, probably the Arctic ecosystem is doing well." Studying these bears is like looking through a window into the entire ecosystem in which they live.

Ever since Steve was a little boy, he wanted to study bears. He read everything he could about them, and when he got a little older, he realized that he wanted to become a wildlife biologist. He went to the University of Washington for a degree in forestry with an emphasis in wildlife management. He earned his master's of science degree focusing on black bears in central Idaho, then joined the United States Fish and Wildlife Service (USFWS) in Wyoming. A position in Alaska opened up. "They wanted someone who knew about bears and could hit the ground running on the Polar Bear Research Project."

"Well," says Steve, giving a quick history of polar bear studies, "people began this research in the sixties, but in those days much of the focus was simply on figuring out how to develop methods that could be used to gather information on polar bears in the Arctic." There was concern that the bears might be jeopardized by heavy hunting in Canada and Alaska.

Before Steve joined the Polar Bear Research Project, the first meeting of what became the Polar Bear Specialist Group for the International Union for Conservation of Nature, or IUCN (the world's main authority on the conservation status of wildlife spe-

The biologist Steve Amstrup with a rare litter of three cubs.

cies), was held in 1965 and was the seed for the International Agreement on Conservation of Polar Bears. This agreement was made in 1973 and renewed in 1981 in perpetuity by all five polar nations: the Soviet Union, the United States, Canada, Denmark, and Norway.

To this day, representatives from the nations who work with polar bears get together to exchange information and collaborate on needed management actions. One of the most important things about this international agreement was that it mandated that shared populations of bears be managed through international consultation. This required that there would be a lot of information sharing among polar bear scientists and managers.

Hunting was coming under control, but at the same time, a new problem became clear: "We became aware," Steve says, "of global warming and the threat it presents to polar bears—a far greater threat because of the extensive loss of essential habitat. You can have a population that is over-harvested, and by reducing the harvest you can allow the population to rebound and grow again. But if a population of animals doesn't have appropriate habitat, then you're in trouble. Because the world is warming (and it's warming because of human influences), there's going to be less sea ice. Sea ice is the habitat of polar bears. The ice is where polar bears have access to their principal prey, which is ringed seals, bearded seals, and spotted and harp seals.

"Polar bears are really only effective in catching seal prey from the surfaces of the sea ice. As the sea ice area declines, the carrying capacity for polar bears also declines. So that's the situation we're in now. Whereas a couple of decades ago our main concern was hunting, now our principal concerns are global warming and habitat loss."

Dr. Steve Amstrup with a captured female and her two-year-old cubs.

Gaylen's job at base camp is to keep the helo (short for *helicopter*) running smoothly so that the biologists can do their sometimes grueling but always exciting work. And now, on the first day of the capture season, Gaylen sits at the computer delving into the AFF website to watch N73LF as it travels across the Beaufort Sea in real time. Joe's helo gives off a GPS reading every eight seconds. In fact, the onboard Geographic Positioning System receiver, or GPS, is finding its location from no fewer than nine satellites at any one time, and the accuracy of the reading is to within fourteen feet of the helo's actual location.

After little more than an hour, the N73LF icon indicates that speed numbers are rising to 5 miles per hour, then 15, now 70, at the same time picking up altitude. Biologists search for bears generally from about three hundred feet above ground level (AGL) and fly at about 75 to 80 knots (86 to 92 mph). When they find a good set of tracks (or a bear), the altitude will drop to between 50 and 100 feet and the speed will drop to between 10 and 50 knots (12–58 mph), depending on how hard it is to follow the tracks.

Gaylen thinks they're following fresh bear prints. Now the speed and altitude suddenly increase. Gaylen, who for hours has been staring at the computer screen, quickly snaps out of a stupor in this overheated building and says, "They're coming in." The icon on the computer map shows the helo making a beeline straight for Barrow at a speed of 90 knots (104 mph) and an altitude of 500 feet.

He throws on his thick Arctic coat and mittens and jumps into the truck.

At the Barrow airport, the helicopter arrives and Gaylen waits patiently for Joe to kill the engine and for the long rotor blades to finally come to rest. Gaylen heads to the helo to begin his inspection routine while Joe goes through his own post-flight checks. Mike and Kristin unload all their gear into the back of the pickup. And it's a lot of stuff: capture duffel bag, capture tool kit, dart kit (toolbox), long duffel with collapsible tripod, engine hoist (for lifting bears), large scale (for weighing bears, which sometimes can be more than 1,300 pounds), dart gun, shotgun, pistols, bear radio collars, tarp and pads, GPS, radio collar VHF (very high frequency) receivers, camera gear, individual food and water for each person, and personal ELTs (emergency locator transmitters). In addition, the helicopter holds emergency survival gear, including a tent, sleeping bags, extra parkas, food, a small stove, an ice ax, a shovel, a snow saw, candles, and signal flares. The survival gear isn't unloaded nightly but remains in the helicopter for the duration of the season. Very rarely, the capture crew gets stuck out on the ice because of bad weather and has to spend a night camped out in the cold. This has happened only once in the nineteen

Gaylen Jensen cleans exhaust smudges off the tail of AStar helicopter N73LF after the completion of a polar bear capture flight.

years that George Durner has been capturing bears.

Once in the truck, Mike says, "We saw lots of bears . . . it was pretty cool. Lots of water, too." During winter and early spring a long "lead" (break in the sea ice) extends from Point Barrow to the northeast for hundreds of miles. Some years this lead is wider than other years, and open water is always present, even during the coldest months of winter. For the last few years Kristin and Mike have noticed that there is more water out there than in the past. The weather and sea ice conditions in any single year are strongly influenced by natural changes in the climate. So far, though, this year's open water cannot be directly linked to the man-caused warming of the planet. Weather is not the same thing as climate. A hot day or a string of hot days, like ice conditions from year to year, can't tell scientists what is happening to the earth's climate. Climate is the sum of weather over long periods of time. Nevertheless, the trends in the Arctic are clear:

Where the southern Beaufort and Chukchi seas meet just north of Barrow, strong currents and winds routinely break the ice apart, forming open water leads and alternately smashing enormous ice pans together to form large pressure ridges of rubble ice. Pressure ridges can sometimes reach almost a hundred feet in height.

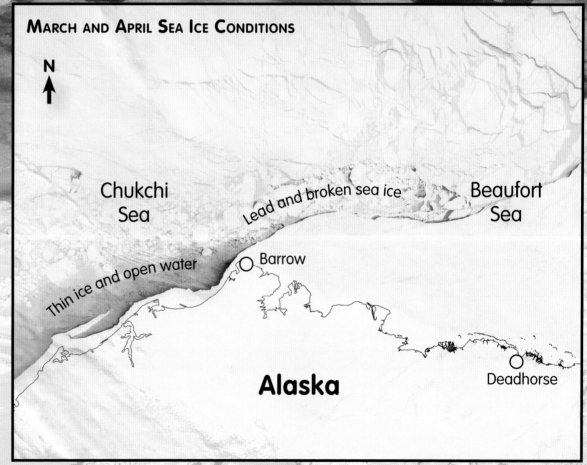

MARCH AND APRIL SEA ICE CONDITIONS

N

Chukchi Sea

Lead and broken sea ice

Beaufort Sea

Thin ice and open water

Barrow

Alaska

Deadhorse

This image illustrates sea ice conditions typical in this region of the Beaufort and Chukchi seas during March and April.

The sea ice is indeed becoming thinner, more unstable, and less expansive. There's less of it, and on average it is unavailable to polar bears for ever-increasing periods of time. That means it is melting and becoming unsafe more quickly than before.

Kristin says, "Today we found a new bear." As with every newly captured bear, the biologists marked him with uniquely numbered ear tags and tattooed the same identifying numbers on the inside of the upper lip on each side of his mouth. Ear tags sometimes get pulled off, but the tattoos remain for the bear's life. Since this was the first bear of the season, the biologists also painted the number 1 on its back. The painted dye number disappears after a few months when the bear sheds its old fur, but it can be seen clearly from the air during the short capture season and prevents the biologists from capturing the same animal twice in the same season.

The dye number 49 on this male indicates that it was the forty-ninth bear caught during the spring capture. Since it was captured once this year, biologists do not need to capture the bear again. This bear, having been caught before, immediately jumped into open water, a common tactic of polar bears to get away from pursuing crews.

The polar bear data sheet Kristin fills out during a capture records key information on each captured bear:

- male or female
- age class (cub born that year, also called a coy; yearling; two-year-old cub; sub-adult; adult). In spring or fall a yearling is a bear that is over a year old but not yet two, typically less than a hundred pounds. Coys are cubs of the year that have just come out of dens in spring, and they are typically less than thirty pounds early in spring.
- markings, such as tattoos, ear tags
- radio collar info
- measurements such as heart girth, neck and skull, total length
- samples taken (blood, serum, fat, milk, ear punch, feces, hair, etc.)

Kristin also marks down what kind of condition the bear is in, whether it's really fat, a 5; or starving, a 1; or any number in between. The second bear they captured today, recorded as a 4, was 635 pounds (288 kg). Kristin also marks down how much wear there is on a bear's teeth, and the presence of scars, cuts, and other physical injuries or abnormalities. She records how many cc of sedative they gave it. This one, being a medium-size bear, got 7 cc of Telazol, a very effective drug that tranquilizes and immobilizes the ani-

mal. It is widely used by other wildlife researchers and veterinarians for research or medical care of carnivores (cc stands for *cubic centimeter* and is the standard medical unit used to determine how much liquid drug is in a given dose). The bear on this day started to wobble twelve minutes after the dart hit it and was down in another six minutes. While the team worked on the bear, it started to wiggle. "We gave him another two cc," Kristin says.

"It can get hectic keeping track of what's going on, especially when you come upon a gaggle of bears, like we did today. I tried to write down where we were finding them, but we kept coming upon more bears, so I gave up."

Mike says, "Unfortunately, most of the bears we saw today we couldn't catch."

Kristin asks, "Did you see that group of five just off the point?" She means Point Barrow, a spit of land just above the town that separates the Chukchi and Beaufort seas. "Five bears!" That was too many too late in the day. You have to dart them all, or none. But Mike and Kristin felt good about getting two bears on their first day out. They have

Biologists take blood samples from an artery that is better exposed under the bear's rear legs.

Telazol is mixed before capture missions and kept in small 30 ml vials. The drug is drawn out by a syringe and put directly into a hollow dart body immediately before the dart is loaded into a dart gun for capture of a bear.

Polar bears are superbly adapted with sharp, short claws to easily cross the roughest of ice pressure ridges.

weeks ahead to capture others. Seasons vary in total number of captures, but seventy to one hundred are typical when working for two months in the southern Beaufort Sea.

In the truck riding back to NARL after the first run of the season, there is much happiness and chitchat and talk of getting pizza as a late dinner for everyone working up the samples and preparing for tomorrow's capture mission. Like a lingering ghost, the spring polar light hangs in the sky at nine-thirty p.m. This far north, the days lengthen quickly in late March, adding about ten minutes of daylight every twenty-

four hours. By the time the Polar Bear Research Project leaves the Arctic in early May, it will be light nearly all the time. A few weeks later, in June, the sun will not set for two months; the great orange ball will sink low to the horizon but then rise up for another day.

As they drive through town, it's easy to see how much Kristin and Mike love their work. This is Kristin's tenth capture season, and Mike has been doing it for nearly that long. Mike says, "I just love being in the field. All the wildlife work has been fun, but I especially love being up here on the ice with the bears."

Mike Lockhart has worked in wild-

life conservation since 1975. During his tenure with the U.S. Fish and Wildlife Service, he participated in a host of research projects on birds of prey; carnivores such as coyotes and badgers; and ungulates—hoofed animals such as mule deer and antelope. He investigated energy development and contaminant and oil spill effects on wildlife, and he developed management responses for potentially affected species. He helped establish a national wildlife refuge near Denver, Colorado. He has also served as the species coordinator for the USFWS endangered black-footed ferret recovery program.

In 2008 he retired after working thirty-three years for USFWS, but he continues to work as a biologist consultant and returns to the Arctic as often as possible to help with the Polar Bear Research Project.

"These bears are such impressive animals," Mike says, smiling. As if to mimic his positive feelings, the people in the streets of Barrow are smiling, too. With the return of the daylight after a long, cold, and dark winter, there is a sense of joy that you can't help but notice when driving through this Iñupiaq Eskimo town. Kids are bombing around on snow machines, running up and down snowbanks. Families gather for late dinners. Everyone is getting ready for whaling season. It's a happy time. The bowhead whales are coming.

Today in fact, from the helo, Joe, Mike, and Kristin spotted an early contingent of bowheads swimming along open leads where polar bears often follow on the ice edge in search of seals. The whales too seem to be coming earlier and earlier in the warming Arctic seas.

Today Mike was the darter and Kristin was the note taker, but over the next six to eight weeks they will take turns at both jobs. While one shoots the tranquilizer darts from the seat behind the pilot, the other sits beside

Wind and moisture can lift ice crystals into the air, often causing an ice rainbow of sorts, called a sun dog.

Mike Lockhart with two yearling bears that are just waking up after being darted, anesthetized, and processed.

21

Joe in the copilot seat, recording data. Today it was Mike's turn to lean out of the helicopter, strapped in with a long harness. Joe took the helo in close, very close, to the running bear, and Mike shot the sedative-filled dart from a distance of maybe ten feet in order to get the dart in the right spot near the shoulder blades at the top of the neck.

Mike explains, "Every once in a while you throw a zinger out there, and it's about five hundred dollars a pop if you miss, but the main reason we get close when darting is to ensure that we get a safe shot. The safe zones are the neck and upper back between the shoulders. You can shoot them lower down on the back or in the butt, but there's more fat there and the drug takes longer to have an effect."

He continues: "It's a little hair-raising sometimes. I do worry about missing or making a bad hit, so that the drug doesn't inject. In such cases you have to go around for another darting run, and you don't want to stress the bear any more than you have to."

Mike grew up in several places across the western United States and now lives in Laramie, Wyoming. He's always

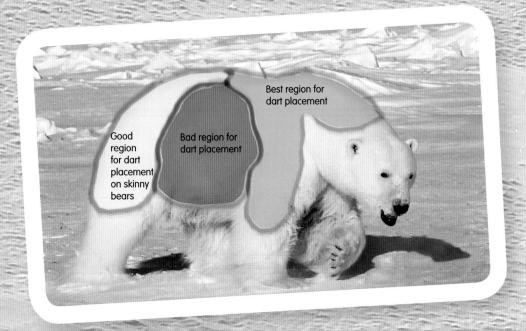

Best region for dart placement

Good region for dart placement on skinny bears

Bad region for dart placement

Polar bear researchers must often capture wild bears to learn more about them. Safe capture depends on drugging the bear through a dart fired from a helicopter. The best places on a bear to receive the dart are on the upper back, shoulder, neck, and forelegs because polar bears have a lot of muscles in these regions. Hitting the bear with a dart in the rump and back legs works well with skinny bears, but on fat bears the drug will be injected into the fat and it can take a long time for the bear to go to sleep. The sides of the polar bear are never darted because there isn't enough muscle there to protect the internal organs. This diagram is courtesy of George Durner.

A large male polar bear walks across ice scoured by wind. Its tracks are obvious in the few patches of soft snow that remain, but they disappear on hard, wind-scoured ice, demonstrating the difficulty biologists often have in tracking bears from a helicopter.

been an outdoorsman. He got involved in the Polar Bear Research Project a decade ago because he and the head of the project, Steve Amstrup, had worked together in the 1970s in Wyoming and Steve knew that Mike had done a lot of aerial survey work for the USFWS. So Steve asked Mike to join him in the field in 2001. Mike has been returning ever since.

Now back at NARL, Mike is washing down the equipment and instruments, the little knives and tools. Gloves need to be cleaned. Sorting through the capture kits and tagging equipment, Mike says, "When we go out, we make a hell of a mess."

He says that one of the bears captured today had two big canine punctures on its face. "Must have been attacked by another male. He had some cuts on his neck, too. They were fresh. But the females? They're usually immaculate. A few years back, we caught a twenty-three-year-old female who was just beautiful and had two fat and healthy two-year-old cubs. You always worry that the male, so much bigger, often twice the size of a female, might hurt her in his love pursuit during mating season,

Mike Lockhart with his arms full of late-spring polar bear cubs. These cubs can be held like this only while anesthetized with the Telazol.

Each night, all the equipment used during the day's capture work has to be thoroughly cleaned and put away for the next mission.

Kristin Simac enters flight and capture data from the day's polar bear capture mission.

Kristin Simac measures and then cuts and bolts together a satellite radio collar to be placed on a suitable female bear when captured. Properly fitted, a satellite collar slips over a bear's head and is comfortable but difficult for the animal to remove.

A hollow dart tip has a short barb to prevent the dart from falling out of the bear once it strikes. The position of the barb is marked to allow easier removal from the bear.

Mike now joins Kristin and Ryan McDonald, a young biology student from the University of Wyoming, in the temporary lab in one of the many buildings at NARL where they have set up all their gear. Here they will process the samples they collected today. They will also enter data from the day's run—from a flight data sheet and a bear data sheet—into a computer, and they will prepare the equipment and darts for tomorrow's run. It is now 10:40 p.m., and their work is just beginning. They're not likely to get to bed until well after midnight.

Kristin Simac has been the key support person for the Polar Bear Research Project on and off in different capacities for ten years. She began as a library runner, then a file clerk, then the gear gatherer. "I still do those things," she says, "but it's kinda nice to be the field biologist now, to know that I can go out and collect the data for scientists like Steve and George, who develop the hypotheses, do the number crunching, the statistical analyses, and the report writing. We collect the data that lead to the results they come up with and their interpretations of that data. Collecting field information is the key piece of the entire process."

Kristin is from Tacoma, Washington. She came to Alaska for a summer vacation in 1984 and never left. She got a job; she got married. She says, "I like living in Anchorage, but it's hard to be away from my extended family in Tacoma." Her bosses—Steve and George back in the USGS offices on the campus of the Alaska Pacific University in Anchorage—used to do a lot more of the capture work, but as they have become extremely busy with the science—and with managing the publicity for such a high-profile animal in light of new debates on climate change—Kristin has freed them up to do more of the analyses and get their findings out the door. In recent years one of the biggest outcomes of this decades-old data collection—and, as Kristin calls it, "their crunching numbers"—was the 2008 designation of polar bears as a threatened species.

but incredibly, these huge males can be extremely gentle with their mates. Once, we saw a male pursuing a female, and when we went in, the male ran off. We processed the female, then went looking for the male. When we came back to check the processed female, we found him lying down next to her, nose to nose, waiting for her to wake up."

THE 2008 THREATENED SPECIES DESIGNATION

Based on the polar bear data collected in a number of locations by the USGS and other agencies from around the world, in May 2008 the U.S. government finally listed polar bears as "threatened"—saying that polar bears could be endangered by midcentury owing to shrinking summer sea ice in a warming Arctic.

Steve Amstrup says, "The trends in polar bear populations over the last several decades are not clear. We know that some populations increased after the International Agreement on Conservation of Polar Bears was signed in 1973. However, there is too little information on many populations to know what their recent trends may have been. Computer modeling, however, projects—based on the recognition that polar bears depend on the sea ice for catching their prey—that a significant global population decline by the middle or end of the century is assured if greenhouse gases are not reduced."

No one truly knows how bad things could get or how fast. But the mere potential for catastrophic effects on any polar bear population is justification enough for action to reduce human-caused greenhouse emissions, which the majority of scientists agree are helping speed up global warming. The polar bear listing may be one of the best catalysts possible for educating the public about climate change effects, and it could possibly help lead to real changes in damaging energy uses and our grossly consumptive lifestyle.

A male polar bear swims in the icy blue waters of an open lead in the ice pack. Polar bears swim by paddling with their front feet alone.

Polar bears will often break through thin ice and into the protection of the ocean to escape capture helicopters. Bears will swim under the ice and periodically lift their heads to take a breath and check to see what's going on above.

A large male bear on pack ice of the Chukchi Sea in 2009.

A Polar Bear Capture

On the dawn of their third day in Barrow, it is −30°F (−34°C). Diamond dust is falling out of the perfect blue sky. That's when tiny flecks of glittering snow crystals are formed in this dry desert climate from the little bit of moisture in the air that comes from open water leads just beyond the land-fast ice west of Barrow. Even on perfectly cloudless days, the microscopic crystals seem to hang in the air like specks of diamonds.

Over a cup of tea, the unflappable helicopter pilot reports, "There's a fog bank five miles off the coast, descending to five hundred feet." Joe continues: "But there's a buffer between here and the coast, five miles give or take. Twenty miles of coastline out to five miles is a pretty good chunk of ice to explore."

Mike says, "Yeah, let's poke around a bit."

Before breakfast, the biologists, the pilot, and the mechanic scrutinize weather conditions to be sure that wind, temperature, and visibility are adequate for undertaking a capture mission. Today the goal is to capture and mark as many bears as possible.

In late spring the sea ice begins to break up, making it impossible to attempt polar bear captures over large expanses of sea ice.

Standard skull length and skull width measurements are taken for every bear captured.

On other days the goal of the biologists might be to find and recover radio collars that have fallen off bears or to target specific bears in order to remove old collars.

At the airport, Gaylen removes the tarp covering the helicopter engine and runs through his safety checks. Mike and Kristin load the helo while Joe steps into the cockpit.

A mild but nevertheless palpable nervousness fills the silence as everyone works to prepare for the capture. The research team will enter a world that is seldom ventured into by humans. "You know about the weather up here," Mike says. "Things can change drastically in a few minutes." That fog bank offshore has everyone a little on edge. But as Kristin says, "It's exciting. You're in

a helicopter; there are incredible creatures before you; there's an excitement in the chase. There's always a little edge to get us going."

Joe volunteered for this job because he really wanted to see polar bears and to fly in the Arctic. He'd already flown many other wildlife capture missions, for grizzly bears, elk, and other species. And he'd flown a lot for mining

Joe Fieldman up close and personal with a large anesthetized cub.

companies, but all his flying in Alaska was farther south, in sub-Arctic reaches of the state. The Arctic is different; it's a more unpredictable environment. He says, "You should never lose sight of the ground. If the fog rolls in, we'll poke around and work our way back. The helicopter is not a stable platform. Helos don't want to stay upright. You take your hands off the controls of a small airplane and it's going to fly in a straight line. You do that with a helicopter and it'll start to veer way over to one side."

Now everyone is on headsets. Voices crackle; the engine fires up. Kristin is in the copilot seat, and Mike is right behind Joe, in a seat where the window slides down enough for him to lean out and dart a bear.

The helo rotor slices the diamond dust. Joe files a flight plan with the tower: "Runway six for departing traffic; altimeter 3015; squawk 1240. Flight plan activated."

Barrow is considered a desert, but on March 27, as the AStar lifts off the icy runway, a thin blanket of snow covers the town, making almost everything white—the surrounding tundra,

The Barrow airport marks the end of sometimes long polar bear capture flights over the pack ice of the southern Beaufort and Chukchi seas.

Flying close to the ground, the helicopter often makes its own blizzard as light ice and snow crystals are picked up in the strong winds created by the powerful rotor blades.

the invisible shoreline, and the ice all the way out to the darker blue of open water leads showing through large cracks in the ice. The ground will be snow covered in the Barrow area for more than another month, and drifts will remain through early summer as the cold Arctic weather prevents the little bit of snow that does fall from melting.

Joe calls to Gaylen to check his radio in the truck. Before he heads back to NARL to monitor the mission on the computer, Gaylen calls back, "Have a good flight."

In a stiffish wind, the helo lifts off like a magic carpet. That's what Joe calls it. In his competent and steady hands, the ride is as smooth as rowing a boat on a mildly choppy pond. Heading northeast

Polar bears often move around the edges of leads, following the ice edge in search of seals. The capture crew searches these areas for bears or their telltale tracks.

along the coast, following the land-fast ice, the crew passes over the "bone pile" just north of town, a place where polar bears congregate in the autumn to feed on unused portions of whale carcasses deposited here during the Iñupiaq fall whale harvest season, when the whales migrate back to the Bering Sea.

Kristin spots the first bear tracks. "Let's see what way they're going," she says.

Joe descends to begin the tracking.

Mike says, "These are old; they're all blown in." Mike and Kristin are both experts at this. Tracking conditions vary immensely. After new snow, tracks are all reasonably fresh. Mike and Kristin study the tracks for sharpness of outline and freshly disturbed snow around the print. If the snow is moist and heavy, they will see the whole paw, especially the toe prints.

After the snow has settled, after winds or days of sun, you might have to get out of the helicopter and check closely to tell how fresh the tracks real-

A fresh dusting of snow over the sea ice makes polar bear tracking easy.

ly are. But in prolonged, stable conditions, tracks can appear fresh for days and you can follow sets for enormous distances. The nice thing about following a good trail is that it often leads to still other tracks that are sometimes even fresher. "Of course," Mike says, "the track itself often tells you what's ahead—a large, independent male or a family group. Tracking can tell you the relative ages of the cubs, too, or even the breeding activity you might come across. You also have to be very careful to check tracks after you're following them for some distance to make sure you're still going in the right direction. Sometimes tracks from multiple bears mix together and you'll take off on a track only to find that you're backtracking another bear. When you follow a good track that leads to a kill site, the bear usually spends a great deal of time there, so it may be up ahead not too far. Finally, sometimes you can tell you're getting really close when the tracks break into a run."

Kristin says, "Wow, a lot of tracks here, but they all look older. Let's head that way." She points east, away from the water.

This female, defensive of her three yearling cubs, actually charged the capture helicopter in an attempt to scare it off. The photo was taken during a polar bear study on the Chukchi Sea by the U.S. Fish and Wildlife Service. Family groups containing three cubs are unusual in the Arctic, especially three cubs that survive their first year of life.

When snow contains enough moisture to compress and pack footprints, winds may subsequently blow away the lighter surrounding snow and leave an elevated print. This is a track that was exposed after winds scoured the bear's path.

An hour out of Barrow, Mike calls, "It's really cold, we're really iced up." He means the windows. "Are there any towels around?" The windows have quickly fogged with the eager breath of the searching capture crew, and the frozen condensation has to be wiped frequently, especially in the back seats. Mike scrapes a little round clear spot in the icy panel of frost.

When tracking conditions are really poor, if the wind blows hard across the ice, scouring the standing snow and obliterating the tracks, or if there are too many tracks all jumbled up together, Mike and Kristin might focus on the ice edges of open leads where polar bears search for seals.

After all his polar bear field seasons, it still amazes Mike how vast the pack ice really is. Pack ice typically covers most of the Arctic oceans in winter months, but it is very dynamic and moves about with ocean currents and winds. Pack ice out over deep ocean water routinely gets split up, creating open leads of water, and it is sometimes forced back together to form pressure ridges and ice rubble fields that are often so large and rough, they would be almost impossible for humans to traverse, but polar bears can do it easily. In the frigid Arctic, open leads of water quickly refreeze, making yet more ice.

A polar bear watches the capture helicopter from the safety of the sea.

The crew follows polar bear tracks that stretch far out in the distance.

Mike is equally amazed at how widely dispersed polar bears can be. "It often feels like we're searching for that proverbial needle in the haystack," he says. On difficult days they will cover hundreds of miles without seeing any bears or fresh tracks. On good days it can be one capture after another and the helicopter uses very little fuel.

The pilot and biologists crane their necks, eyes seared by the polar light reflecting off all that white below, looking all around, expecting some chunk of ice to move, suddenly transforming itself into an animal: the biggest bear in the world! A white bear on a white background!

No one spots a bear for hours. Lots of open water, though. Joe says, "Wow, look how the ice has opened up."

Kristin says, "Yeah, bad news. What a mess." She means that where the ice hits the open water, it's all jumbled, a scramble of dicey ice; it's no place to capture bears.

Joe keeps the helo running slowly along the edge of the lead up the coast, and suddenly Mike spots a set of fresh tracks. Bears don't follow straight paths for long. They explore. Joe goes down so far that he actually blows in the tracks from the blade of the helo. "Brilliant," he says of his own error.

Joe jokes, "He's probably watching us as we speak."

Just when they think they'll never spot a bear today, Mike calls out, "Got one. Three o'clock."

And bingo—there's the running bear, a massive animal scampering over the lopsided ridges of jumbled ice. It's a big male, too. Really big.

Joe calls out, "So you wanna push him behind us or into the rubble in the other direction?"

The Arctic sea is a wondrous, magical, and ever-changing environment of ice, weather, and water.

Kristin says, "Not sure the ice is thick enough out there. Let's push him over to the right."

Once a bear is found, the team assesses whether it's safe for both the bear and the crew to attempt a capture run. Bears cannot be darted if there's any chance at all that they could reach open water after the tranquilizer takes effect. In fact, many capture efforts are aborted because of nearby open water or thin ice. Thick ice can usually be determined from the air as it is typically whiter, with more surface texture; thin ice has a blue-water cast and is smoother.

This bear is sufficiently clear of open water, and the ice is thick enough to make the capture.

Mike gauges the size of the bear to determine the amount of tranquilizer to use in the dart before he puts the dart in the gun. This guy is maybe a thousand pounds, so the maximum 10 cc (.3 ounces) of Telazol is needed. Females, usually half this size, get 7 cc; two-year-old cubs get 5 cc; and yearlings get 3.

Great care is taken to minimize stress on the animal. Under perfect conditions a darting attempt is accomplished quickly and effectively so that the bear is drugged and goes down after only a couple of minutes in an open area that

facilitates close landing and easy handling and processing.

Mike says, "Straight ahead will be fine. I'm going to wait to load up until we know we have him where we want him."

There is palpable excitement in the helo as Joe zeros in and begins to herd the bear toward a wide, flat expanse of ice. Although this bear does not seem inclined to head for open water, Kristin is concerned about some large cracks she's spotted that run through the ice nearby; some of them might mean water.

There are many things that contribute to an effective darting run, says Mike. The dart gun itself must be care-

A large male polar bear is herded to a smooth area in the ice for processing.

Mike Lockhart loads an immobilizing dart with Telazol immediately before a capture attempt.

fully "sighted in," or test-fired, to make sure the gun is shooting accurately and consistently before the biologist tries to dart bears from the air. All the dart pieces and the charges that propel the dart have to be pretested to be sure everything is working correctly. There is an internal charge inside the dart that must go off properly in order to inject the sedative into the bear. The size and speed of the bear, its behavior, its response to the helicopter, and the nature of the terrain also affect the dart run. It can be challenging from the window of a moving helicopter to dart a weaving and dodging bear running at full speed. That's why having a pilot as skilled and experienced as Joe Fieldman is so important for the safety of the crew and the bear.

Mike says, "I'm loading up."

Joe counters, "Give me another thirty seconds, Mike." He continues to herd the bear without scaring it too much; the helo hovers rather high up as he does it. The bear stumbles up a pressure ridge. Mike now loads the dart gun with the long dart that carries the Telazol.

The field biologist starts to take aim as Joe Fieldman maneuvers the helicopter over a running polar bear. To ensure proper placement of the dart, the bear is not darted until the helicopter is directly over it.

Three different length dart tips are used to capture bears. Although all look long and somewhat dangerous, they cause little harm to polar bears, who have thick hides and massive fat and muscle.

35

As the helicopter descends to fifty feet above the ice, the rotor creates a mushrooming plume of snow that temporarily envelops the polar bear. At twenty-five feet the snow plume passes the bear, giving the pilot and crew a clear view of the ice and the animal. Now Joe maneuvers the helo right above the body of the running bear; and secured in his harness, Mike lowers his window to lean halfway out. His face is suddenly hit with the blast of –20° wind, and his ears are assaulted by the roar of the helicopter blades spinning overhead. The inside of the helo is chaotic, cold, and loud, with blowing wind and the whirl of the rotor. Joe drops to within ten feet of the running bear's back. The bear swivels and for a second seems to think about giving a fight, but it turns and keeps running.

Mike's microphone is "hot," meaning that he talks with Joe to help Joe place the helicopter in the best possible position for darting the bear. Because of this, Joe and Kristin also hear in their headphones the outside roar of the rotor blades and the rush of wind. Mike takes aim; the ocular sight on the darting gun places a small orange triangle on the shoulder of the running bear. Mike steadies the triangle on the bear's shoulder and pulls the trigger. The dart

A female polar bear and her two cubs, recently emerged from their snow den, were encountered while moving out to the far pack ice to find seal prey. As soon as the cubs are old enough to follow, the mother bear must return to the sea to seek food. She has been fasting during the entire birthing and early cub-rearing period and has not eaten for several months. The body fat that she carried with her into the den has sustained her cubs, but in early spring she must restore her fat to ensure her cubs' survival as well as her own.

flies true and hits the bear exactly on the shoulder.

"Nice shot," Joe calls as he backs way off to let the drug take effect. He pulls away from the bear and circles the helo from about three hundred feet away and three hundred feet high. Maintaining this distance calms the bear somewhat; it stops running and either walks or just stands and watches the circling helicopter.

Occasionally Mike or Kristin will get a female protecting her cubs that's very aggressive and actually tries to grab the helicopter. Last year they came dangerously close when a female turned, jumped, and came within inches of grabbing their helicopter's strut. The pilot pulled up just in time.

Kristin is recording the time of the hit and the location of the dart on the bear (left shoulder), and everyone in the helo is keeping a close eye on the animal to make sure it doesn't head for any open water. This bear is very strong. He walks for a good five minutes before he begins to falter. First he stumbles on a block of ice, then keeps running. But in another minute or so, the big male staggers, drops its back end, stands up again, fighting the sedative, then drops down slowly, flat out on the ice, immobilized, eyes open and breathing deeply.

A darted young male polar bear begins to appear sleepy as the Telazol takes effect.

A darted polar bear slumps on the ice as the drug from the dart takes effect. When a polar bear is completely lying down, it is safe to land the helicopter nearby and begin all the associated processing.

37

As gently as he can, Joe lowers the AStar and lands right near the bear so the biologists can begin the processing.

But not all captures are so simple. Mike, who is still in the helicopter putting away the darting gear when the rotor blades come to rest, says, "If it's a breeding pair, we'll sedate the female first and then the male. If it's a family group and if the cubs are two-year-olds, we'll dart them all from the air, mom first, then each of the offspring. If it's a group of one-year-olds or cubs of the year, we'll sedate the mom, and after she goes down, we'll converge on the cubs from the ground." The normal pattern is to land the helo a respectful distance from the mom to ensure that the cubs don't run, and while the engine is kept running, the biologists get out and try to either hand capture the new cubs or dart yearlings from the ground.

For protection during ground darting of yearling bears, one biologist carries a shotgun loaded with a low-velocity beanbag charge to discourage a potentially aggressive cub from attacking. Lethal rounds follow in the magazine for the unlikely event that the beanbag doesn't stop an attack. Mike explains further: "The shotgun used for protection has an extended magazine that holds six rounds. We intentionally take one of the lethal rounds out and put in a much less powerful round that has a small beanbag that will sting the bear

Yearling bears are often darted from the ground while the helicopter hovers in the distance, ready to herd the bears back to mom if they start to run away before they can be darted.

A cub of the year being held before being given a drug shot that will put it to sleep for a short period.

and not cause injury. No bears have been killed in self-defense during capture efforts over the thirty years of the Beaufort Sea project."

If the cubs run off during ground capture attempts, Joe lifts off to herd them back to their mom. Mike recalls one time when he and Steve Amstrup were out together. They thought the little ones were yearlings, but it turned out they were two-year-olds, and they ran off. The pilot had to drive them back.

As Kristin pulls duffels and waterproof cases from the helicopter storage compartments and walks them over to the bear, she says, "Cubs usually stick with the mom. But last year two cubs went different ways. One of us went on foot to try to keep track of one cub while the other biologist went in the helicopter to find the other. Then we all had to re-find each other. I usually never leave the area around the helicopter, but on that day the helo wandered off a mile or two, looking for a cub. I put on my yellow helmet so the pilot could find me again."

No matter how many times he's done this before, when Mike first comes up to a new bear, that incredible creature lying on the ice, eyes open, breathing, diamond dust sparkling above, there's nothing like it in the world, he says. "What beauty!"

With the bear fully under the effect of the tranquilizer, Kristin removes the dart, checks how much of the drug was actually injected into the bear, and records details of drug dosing on a capture data form. Sometimes additional

This cub was captured at the same time as its mother. Both bears were weighed and measured to learn more about their health and growth.

As the capture helicopter approaches a darted female polar bear, her cub of the year cautiously peeks out from her protection.

sedative is administered before work gets under way. But not with this bear.

After taking initial photos, Mike, Kristin, and Joe settle into some serious work. There's much to do. First, the bear is repositioned to keep its head out of the deeper snow so that it can breathe more freely. If the bear is facing toward the sun, the face is covered to keep the sun out of the drugged bear's open eyes.

The bear is then rolled onto its belly on a tarp with Therm-a-Rest pads placed underneath it to fully insulate it from contact with snow and ice. If the bear is wet, it is dried off with towels. Vitals—respiration and temperature—are taken. If a bear is too hot—more than 103°F (39°C)—snow is applied to vascular areas in the groin and armpits so that the body temperature lowers before anything else is done.

The first test Mike and Kristin perform on this bear is known as BIA, or bioelectrical impedance analysis, which is a method for estimating body fat composition. For polar bears, fat is where it's at. Fat polar bears are better able to survive long periods when the hunting may not be good. Also, a very fat pregnant bear will be more likely to be successful in having and raising cubs than a bear that does not have enough fat. Hence, knowing the "fatness" of polar bears provides scientists with very important information on the health of these animals.

A bear is spread out on pads to administer a BIA test.

Measurements are taken before a male bear recovers from drug effects. Biologists try to complete their work using as little of the immobilizing drug as possible so that the bears will wake quickly and not be vulnerable to other bears that are potentially roaming nearby.

BIOELECTRICAL IMPEDANCE ANALYSIS (BIA)

BIA is taken by placing two needles at the base of the bear's tail and connecting electrodes to those needles and to a measuring device that also has electrodes attached to the lips. There are right and left electrodes that can't be crossed. BIA determines the electrical impedance, or opposition to the flow of an electric current through body tissues, which can then be used to estimate total body water (TBW). TBW helps calculate fat-free body mass and, by comparing its difference with body weight, body fat. BIA is taken before any sampling occurs, in order to maximize the efficiency of the test.

Joe has proved to be invaluable, and not just as a pilot. He actively participates in all bear processing work. He now grabs a clipboard and begins to write while Kristin and Mike call out measurements. Joe helps with rolling the bear over and takes many of the standard measurements himself. He also assists with the markings and taking of biological samples.

Scars on the face of this big male show that he's been in a few fights with other bears.

Bears have to be rolled onto their back, stomach, and sides for the scientists to take various measurements and samples. Now this bear is on its back and deeply under the sedative's influence, with the underside of its rear legs well exposed for taking blood. (Also, this is one of the best positions for getting a milk sample from a lactating female. If the biologists encounter a female that has cubs, at the onset of processing they administer a shot of oxytocin, a hormone that induces lactation and, for biologists, makes milk collection easier.)

The immense size of this bear's paws reflects the power it would have should it wake from its sleep.

Once the biologists are down on the ice working on a bear, it is nearly impossible to imagine just how much the ice beneath them could be changing or moving in the strong currents. Often they work on foot-thick plates of ice that stretch for dozens of miles in all directions. The local Iñupiaq Eskimos, ice experts because they have hunted here for thousands of years, have hundreds of separate names for different ice conditions and various ice formations.

Kristin calls out and Mike repeats, "Bear 20649." Kristin is reading the faded number on the lip tattoo as she

A hefty male polar bear is positioned on dry air mattresses to perform a BIA test—a physiological test that reveals the bear's relative body fat content—an important indicator of overall health.

Biologists take blood samples from a sedated polar bear.

The polar bear's claws are short and stocky compared with those of the grizzly bear, the better for walking on ice and gripping heavy prey such as seals. The claws are sharp and deeply scooped on the underside to assist in digging in the ice.

opens the bear's mouth, revealing his massive canine teeth.

This bear is a recapture from 2003. Kristin is checking the big book they carry with them in the field, a record of all bear captures from the past. She discovers that this was the eighty-first bear of that year, and no one has seen him since. He was 950 pounds in 2003. He'll be weighed further along in the process to see if he's gained or lost weight, but he looks a little thin for his size.

The bear is rolled onto his side. This is where the most important tagging takes place—the lip tattooing given to every bear captured for the first time. The tattoo is applied with a punch instrument that forces permanent ink into patterns of small holes under the skin of the inside of the upper lip on both sides of the bear's mouth. The small holes punched harmlessly into the gums form dotted patterns of unique numbers that permanently identify this individual bear. Since both tattoos on Bear 20649 are difficult to read, he has to be re-marked. Tattoos have to be applied carefully, and they can be illegible if the team member doesn't get a proper grip on the gum or get enough ink in the small punch holes. Having numbers on both gums increases the chances of a good, readable tag.

While Kristin takes responsibility for tattoos today, Mike and Joe conduct side measures and complete biological samples. Measurements include skull length and total length (for which the bear has to be moved into in a resting position). A vestigial premolar is extracted, if needed. This is a small tooth that has become dysfunctional during the course of polar bear evolution; *vestigial* means that the bears don't use it anymore. To get the tooth, the biologists use two tools: an elevator, which is a probe that helps loosen the tooth in the socket, and a pair of grooved tooth extractors, specialized pliers that grab the tooth and help it come out more easily.

The head of each bear is supported when the bear is lowered by the tripod used to weigh bears. Holding the head up keeps the bear's mouth and nose out of the snow and allows for freer breathing.

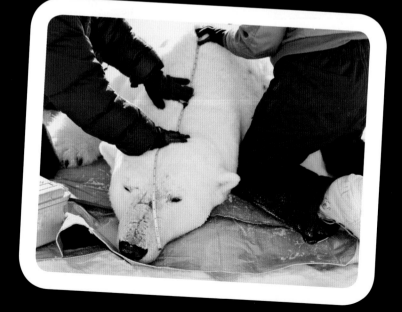

To begin processing, bears are first spread out on mats for the BIA test. In addtion to the BIA, several other measurements and samples that are best taken while the bear is on its belly can also be accomplished immediately following the BIA work.

It takes three people to roll this bear off the tarp and onto its belly for a series of other measurements and markings. The bear is moved into a straight line, its fore and rear feet positioned carefully in a relaxed manner.

Bears captured for the first time also get unique ear tags. Ear tags may be retained over the life of a female, but males routinely lose them during fights with other bears. This big guy is missing his left ear tag. Ear tags are white and are not obvious except under relatively close inspection.

The crunch of the snow is loud as Joe, Kristin, and Mike keep working on the bear. Occasionally they glance around to see if any other bears might be near and have grown curious about what's happening.

"Hold the tail here," Mike says, and calls out, "Eight point six feet [262 cm] total length; seven point six feet [232 cm] standard length." Kristin rubs a separate cotton swab between the toes of the bear's rear and front feet for scientists at the San Diego Zoo who are studying bear scent behavior. Mike

takes a fat biopsy and then collects some hair and feces.

Joe continues to write down notes:
- Heart girth: 165 cm (5.4 feet)
- Skull width: 25.2 cm (10 inches)
- Skull length: 43.7 cm (17.2 inches)
- Tail: 14 cm (6 inches)

During the entire processing time the bear is examined for recent and old physical scars, abnormalities, and tooth condition, all of which are recorded. This bear's body condition is rated 3 out of 5, because he's not that hefty for his size. Tooth wear (for the bear's low-

Scent samples are swabbed from between the toes of polar bears and sent to biologists at the San Diego Zoo who are studying polar bear scent behavior.

A different measure of a bear's total length is taken for biological impedance analysis (BIA). The length compared with data obtained from BIA electrode readings provides a relative understanding of the bear's body fat and health.

Biologists take a breath sample from an anesthetized bear. Breath samples provide stable isotope data that can be used to determine what the bear has been eating.

er incisors) rates 2 out of 3; old scars on the bear's face rate a 3; fresh cuts on his entire body all rated 1 out of 3, meaning negligible.

Kristin does a breath sample by fitting a cup over the bear's muzzle. The cup has a one-way valve attached to a heavy plastic bag that captures the breath. Breath samples are taken from every recent bear captured, to give scientists at the University of Wyoming data to help determine what bears have been feeding on. Over the many years the Polar Bear Research Project has been capturing polar bears, some kinds of samples taken in the field have changed while some of the basic sampling—all the measurements, blood, fat, ear punch, hair, feces—have remained the same. Pedal and nasal swabs and BIA were samples added in recent years for each capture.

Now for the weighing. Mike holds the big fella's arm up as he's first rolled onto the nylon net that is attached to an electronic scale that can measure weights up to 2,000 pounds. Then the biologists lift the bear slowly by the engine hoist and chain connected to a portable tripod. This great white sleeping beast is hoisted above the ice, and there's an amazing tenderness from the biologists

All information and measurements for each captured bear are carefully recorded on field data sheets.

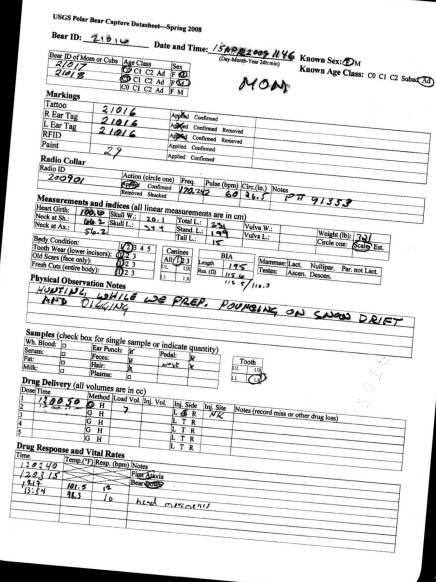

45

for the bear. They will hold his head, rather than just let it dangle, as he is hoisted in the net. This bear weighs in at 995 pounds, for a net weight gain of 45 pounds since he was last weighed, in 2003. The increase in weight is a good thing.

Joe says, "Want a hand?"

Now it takes all three of them to roll this guy on his stomach again. The icy wind is strong and picking up speed as the bear's massive head begins to quiver and rise a little above the green tarp. Forty-five minutes after the first dart went into the bear with the max of 10 cc of Telazol, its whole body begins to shake and get a little squirrelly. Mike pops two more cc of Telazol into the big boy so he and Kristin can finish their work.

At the very end, while the bear is still on his stomach, temperature and respiration are checked again before departure, and the bear's drug response is recorded. They want to be sure he is showing signs of waking. Mike paints a big blue 3 on the bear's back.

Processing the bear lasts about an hour and fifteen minutes. Once all data are recorded and sampling procedures completed, Mike and Kristin

After all the measurements and samples are taken, each bear is marked with a temporary dye number to clearly identify it from the air. The number prevents biologists from recapturing that bear during the same season.

George Durner weighs a large male polar bear. A collapsible metal tripod, engine hoist, and net are used to hoist bears off the ground and get an accurate weight via an attached electronic scale.

return the processing equipment to the helicopter. In most cases, drugged bears display initial signs of waking (head and limb movements) just as the biologists are leaving. Bears that are under the effect of drugs can be especially vulnerable to attack by other bears, so to ensure that drugged bears remain safe, upon departure the crew will fly concentric circles around each captured bear for up to a half mile to check for the presence of other bears.

When all the gear is collected and safely stored in the helo, Joe fires up the engine, first making sure that all the doors are secure. As the AStar lifts off the ground like a feather floating into the air, the big bear starts to move a bit. Blowing snow rushes by him and he blinks as he watches the helicopter rise into the sky. Soon he will be on his feet, a big number 3 painted on his back, and he will go about his work of hunting seals.

As the effects of Telazol wear off, polar bears first move the head and then groggily rise up on their front legs. Full recovery usually follows soon afterward.

A Conversation with Dr. Steven Amstrup About Capture-Recapture Population Estimates and Polar Bears

"Most of what we know about polar bears we know from capturing them and then releasing them alive at the site of capture," says Steve. "Early on, the pioneers in polar bear research realized that polar bears couldn't be counted very effectively by flying over them. It really is difficult to spot a white bear in a white environment."

The result is that every year or almost every year since the late 1960s the Polar Bear Research Project has gone out into the field to capture bears. Steve says, "Whenever you catch them, you measure them, you weigh them, you do all kinds of things. But most important, you mark them. Then you go out the next year and catch a bunch more bears, and most of them are unmarked, but some are ones you marked the previous year. You can understand what the physical condition of the animal is, and over time you can learn whether captured bears' conditions are changing. Are they larger now or smaller, or fatter now, or skinnier than they used to be?"

In its simplest form, a capture-recapture estimate is the ratio of the number of bears in the population that are marked versus those that are unmarked. Through a variety of assumptions and statistical techniques, scientists use the relationship between the number of previously captured and tagged bears in a sample with the number and status of newly captured, unmarked bears to assess changes in overall population level, birth rates, survival, and animal conditions.

Steve says that populations of wild animals fluctuate over time anyway. Right now scientists are concerned about changes in population that might be caused by loss of sea ice habitat from global warming. "What we've learned from the last forty years will help us project what's likely to happen in the next forty years. If the data were perfectly clean, you could run models that have been around since the fifties with a pad of paper and a hand calculator. Unfortunately, in the real world of wildlife research, nothing is simple. And in order to get the best estimates, we have to engage all of the modern statistical techniques that are now possible because of the power of personal computers."

For many years Steve has consulted with Trent McDonald of Western EcoSystems Technology (WEST) in Laramie, Wyoming, for this kind of statistical expertise. WEST is contracted to help analyze Steve's data, and the company often suggests new and different ways to collect information in the field that will help with the overall analysis. "There's lots of give-and-take between the project and the consultant," says Steve. It's a process of fine-tuning the collection of data and the application of statistical tests.

Biologists enter biological sample data and flight event data from the day's capture of bears.

A female bear placed on insulating mats and a tarp for a BIA test is also refitted with a new satellite-radio collar. This female has been wearing a collar for more than two years (note the compressed hair on its neck), but a fresh collar with new batteries will enable even more data to be gathered on her movements and sea ice use for many months to come.

Another Capture

The team is back in the air searching for tracks again.

An hour goes by before Kristin spots a female running along some rough ice.

Joe says, "We have two choices. We can push her all the way through this rough stuff and get her to where it starts to be more solid, or we can go toward that big ice pan over there, where it opens up."

Kristin asks, "Should we dart her and then push her that way?" She points away from the open water. With water fairly close by, darting this bear will not be quite so straightforward as the last one.

Joe says, "I'll get her over this rough stuff." Then everyone agrees on a good spot.

Mike loads the dart into the gun.

Joe calls out, "Ready, Mike?"

Mike says, "I'm getting there," and when Mike's dart gun is loaded, he opens the window and leans way out on his harness, dart gun pointed at the running bear.

Joe takes them down close to the bear and calls out, "We're on her."

Mike again steadies the gun, bringing the orange triangle of the ocular sight over the bear's shoulder. He calmly aims for and hits his target, making it look so simple. Having a great pilot with a steady hand helps a lot. In fact, it all looks like child's play. Already this team of skilled biologists and pilot work well together, as if they've done this for decades, yet it's only the third day of a long capture season, with many such days ahead, when the weather and bears might not cooperate so well.

After the dart strikes the bear, the helo backs off two hundred feet to the side. Soon the bear staggers and slumps to the ice—much more quickly than the big male earlier in the day. She looks half the size, maybe under five hundred pounds. Mike used a dart with only 7 cc (.2 ounces) of Telazol, a typical amount for a female.

In a matter of minutes Joe has the AStar sitting fifty feet from the immobilized bear, with the rotors coming to a full stop. Out piles the gear.

Gear is brought out from the helicopter to measure, weigh, and sample this female polar bear. She wears a radio collar that was put on her when she was captured well over a year earlier.

After checking the dart and the bear's vitals, Kristin is looking for a clear ID, because this is a recapture. The female has an ear tag, a lip tattoo, and a satellite-radio collar.

"There it is: bear ID 20925," calls Kristin. Looking in the record book, she sees that this female was captured in a completely different area on April 9, 2008, and that she got everything all at once that day—tattoo, ear tags, collar. The book shows that last year this bear had two coys with her, yet now, when she normally should have them with her, she has none. The cubs should still be traveling with their mother at this age. The biologists do not know what happened to the cubs, but this is not the first time they have seen such loss.

The big data book is supposed to be consulted to see if everything checks out (for example, if a tooth sample was taken in a previous capture). There is talk about simplifying this cross-referencing in

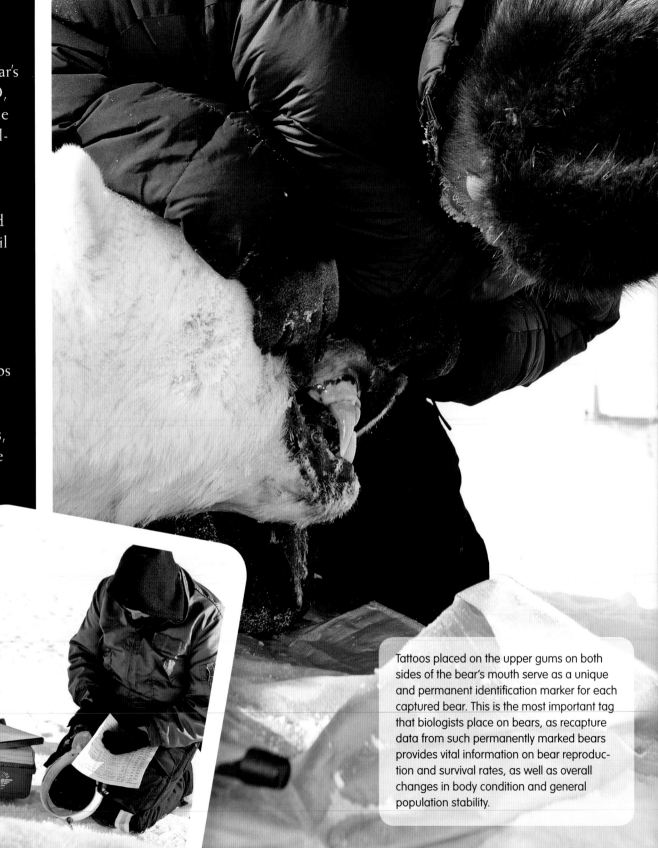

Each satellite collar has to be turned on, the frequency checked, and the serial number recorded before it is fitted on a polar bear.

Tattoos placed on the upper gums on both sides of the bear's mouth serve as a unique and permanent identification marker for each captured bear. This is the most important tag that biologists place on bears, as recapture data from such permanently marked bears provides vital information on bear reproduction and survival rates, as well as overall changes in body condition and general population stability.

the field by putting the whole database on some kind of electronic device, but today Kristin and Mike still carry the large population database book.

This bear also wears an RFID (radio frequency identification) ear tag in one ear. The RFID tag, which is different from simple plastic ID ear tags, has a small transmitter that emits a short-range VHF radio signal that can be picked up with a special receiver and RFID antennas attached to the bottom of the helicopter, but you have to be close for the RFID equipment to work. The RFID radio signal includes a unique bar code for each bear. The idea is that you can check the RFID gear the following year and see if it is a previously captured bear that does not need to be recaptured. RFID tags have the potential to supplement the mark-recapture database because the device allows researchers to identify bears in the field remotely.

Satellite transmitters do something entirely different from RFID tags—they give movement data on individual bears with accurate locations—so a bear's habitat use and distribution over time can be tracked. Several new satellite transmitters are now being tested. One is a smaller ear tag radio and another is a glue-on transmitter attached to the fur on the bear's back. The glue-on and ear tag satellite radios do not have VHF

beacons, so they cannot be used to identify bears in the field. In effect, they give a bigger picture of bear behavior and movements.

Because this female has been caught so recently, she doesn't need any ID tags or tattoos today. The biologists will, however, conduct the usual tests—blood, fat, measurements, and so on. For just under an hour they work in the frigid bright light.

Each polar bear radio collar contains a satellite GPS and a VHF radio transmitter. This VHF receiver is onboard the helicopter, which also has special directional antennas, and is used to find radio-collared polar bears. Under proper conditions, this receiver can pick up a signal from many miles away and the helicopter crew can home in on the bear's location by flying in progressively smaller box patterns. As they come closer to the bear, the signal gets stronger.

53

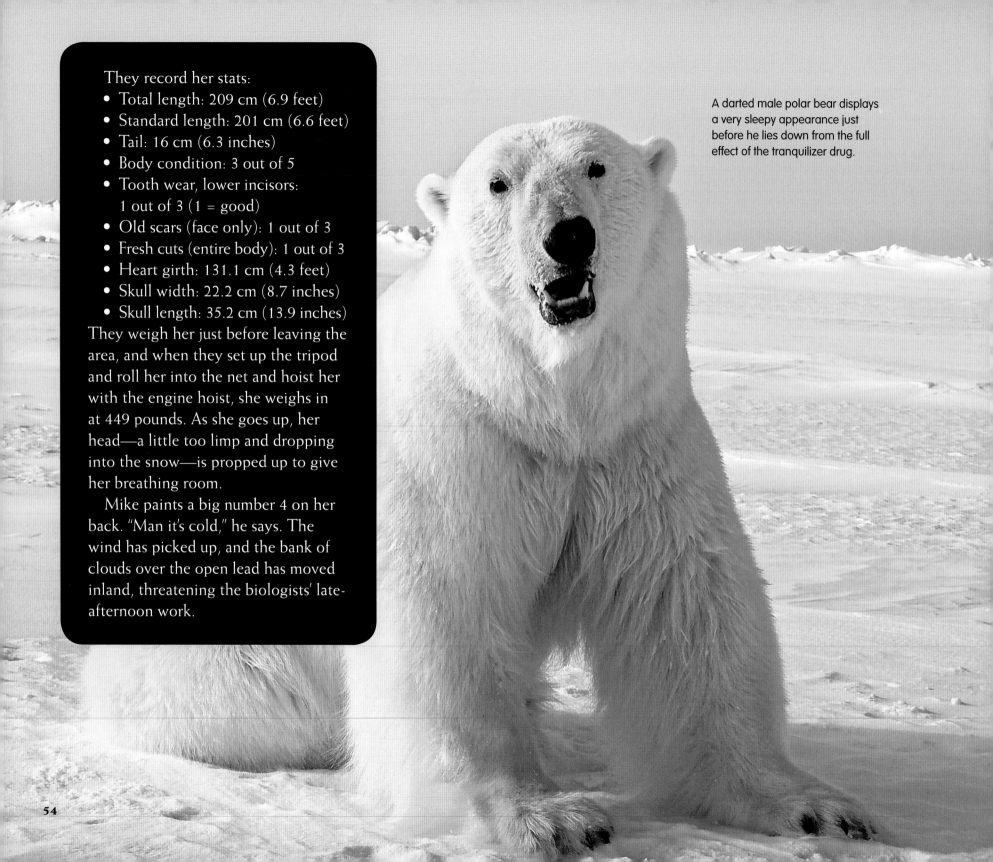

They record her stats:
- Total length: 209 cm (6.9 feet)
- Standard length: 201 cm (6.6 feet)
- Tail: 16 cm (6.3 inches)
- Body condition: 3 out of 5
- Tooth wear, lower incisors:
  1 out of 3 (1 = good)
- Old scars (face only): 1 out of 3
- Fresh cuts (entire body): 1 out of 3
- Heart girth: 131.1 cm (4.3 feet)
- Skull width: 22.2 cm (8.7 inches)
- Skull length: 35.2 cm (13.9 inches)

They weigh her just before leaving the area, and when they set up the tripod and roll her into the net and hoist her with the engine hoist, she weighs in at 449 pounds. As she goes up, her head—a little too limp and dropping into the snow—is propped up to give her breathing room.

Mike paints a big number 4 on her back. "Man it's cold," he says. The wind has picked up, and the bank of clouds over the open lead has moved inland, threatening the biologists' late-afternoon work.

A darted male polar bear displays a very sleepy appearance just before he lies down from the full effect of the tranquilizer drug.

Time for the biologists on the Polar Bear Research Project to depart. Everything is quickly packed into the AStar, and Joe lifts it off the ground. Fighting off the sedative, bear 20925 scrambles to get up. Joe makes a few passes to look for any bears nearby. None. And back to the base they fly to work in the lab. After a day of captures, there's still a lot of essential work to be done.

Joe Fieldman blocks the sun with his body while his arms stretch toward atmospheric ice crystals that form small rainbows on the horizon. These atmospheric displays, called sun dogs, in this case could more appropriately be called Joe dogs.

A Conversation with Dr. Steven Amstrup About Radio Collars and Polar Nations

The International Polar Bear Treaty says that shared populations will be studied and managed through consultation. So if there is a group of bears that move back and forth between Canada and Greenland, for example, the treaty says that the bears need to be managed jointly by the two nations. "You can't do that unless you share your research," Steve says. "If we don't take advantage of what others are doing, we'll be continually reinventing the wheel. For example, I was the first person in the early 1980s to successfully radio collar polar bears and follow them around the sea ice." Other polar nations soon began to attach radio collars to their bears to learn how they interact with the sea ice and prey distribution.

There are many similarities in the kinds of radio tags applied to all polar bears. Steve says, "The kind of collar or radio tag you attach depends a lot on the objective of a particular study. For example, one of our ongoing studies is to try to understand how polar bears are using their habitats when they're stuck on land, compared with habitats out on the sea ice. In order to help understand foraging patterns and relationships to different kinds of habitats, we might want detailed, even hourly records of where the bear traveled and how much movement

A couple of the essentials for the day's capture flight are loaded into the helicopter. Satellite transmitters readied for use and a pistol worn by biologists for protection against bears (which have never been used for defense on this project) are taken out during daily capture flights.

there was. That objective calls for a transmitter that transmits frequently at a high rate, so that you get a number of transmissions every hour or at least every day. On the other hand, if what you are really interested in is how this bear is moving throughout the years—that is, does it use the same kind of habitats every year?—then you might want to use a transmitter that transmits once or twice a week but will last a long time. There is always a tradeoff. If you have a collar that gives you a lot of information, it will go through its battery life much faster than one that transmits only once or twice a week. So you might get six months of very intensive data from dozens of locations per day from one kind of collar, or you might have a collar that lasts three years but gives only one or two locations a week."

What is done with all this data?

"We spend two or three months in the field, but the rest of the year we're back in the office analyzing data and writing reports. So the kind of collar or radio tag we deploy will also guide the kind of analysis we do later." Often scientists do that initial study and then realize that they could look at their data in a different way, which might tell them something they hadn't even thought of. "So you can't necessarily say at the very beginning what all the uses of a particular data stream are likely to be," says Steve.

"The amount of data we're getting from polar bears now is phenomenal. The radio tags and collars are transmitting not just location. Some out there tell us whether a bear is in the water or not; some tell us such things as the bear's activity (moving or resting), or its body temperature. The collars and tags send a lot of information, which amounts to lots and lots of space on computer hard drives. Fortunately, at the same time that radio tags have been advancing, our computers are advancing, too, and that gives us the ability to store and manage huge volumes of data."

Dr. Steve Amstrup at his Anchorage office. Years of data gathered in the field are followed by years of analysis in the offices of scientists like Steve and George Durner. These analyses are key to learning how polar bears live and move over the habitats they need to survive, and how the populations are responding to a rapidly changing world.

Fresh batches of Telazol are made every few days to replace the amount used during previous capture missions.

Recording Information

At NARL, Kristin and Ryan start to log data and bag and label all the samples, preparing them for storage and future analyses. Data from the bear data sheets and the flight data sheets have to be entered into the computer.

Mike works on cleaning and preparing all the gear for the next day's capture. First he has to clean the dart gun and the charge insert, and, if they are needed, he has to prep new darts and mix more Telazol. The guns are unloaded and locked away for storage. Then all the other work: thermometers, tattoo pliers and inserts, ear punch pliers, knives, blood shuttles, tooth extractors, collar tools, tape measures, calipers, spent dart components—all have to be washed, sterilized, and put into their proper containers for easy access tomorrow. Although it is very cold out in the field, everything gets typically soaking wet when brought inside, and many tools are covered with tattoo ink, fur dye, and small amounts of blood. In addition, the biologists use multiple pairs of gloves and towels in the field that get filthy and have to be washed (at least every other day or so),

Capture dart parts. A number of dart bodies of varying doses have to be prepared before each bear capture outing.

Kristin Simac reconstitutes dried Telazol powder to make the drug for polar bear captures. Telazol is mixed only as needed for the next day's capture work.

The Polar Bear Research Project leader, George Durner, is in charge of enormous volumes of polar bear population data that have been gathered over the last thirty years.

along with a blanket used to insulate small cubs of the year. The weighing tripod, also usually wet, has to be broken down and allowed to dry out; otherwise, when it goes out the next day, it could freeze and be very difficult to assemble. Similarly the scale and hoist are air-dried.

The biological sampling kits have to be refurbished with whirl packs, blood tubes, surgical gloves, swabs, vials, fat punches, and forceps. All the contents of the large "capture bag" have to be removed and the duffel turned inside

out so that everything can dry overnight. The capture duffel carries the gloves, towels, cub rope, blanket, fur-dying materials, large clippers, the BIA kit, and so forth. The "dart kit," a plastic toolbox, has to be checked to ensure that there are enough prepped darts of each size and enough dart charges and syringes (for loading darts). The "capture kit," another toolbox, includes bear ear tags and ear-tagging tools, all the tattooing tools, measuring instruments, thermometers, syringes, blood shuttles, tooth extractors, and collar wrenches.

"All this stuff has to be cleaned and laid out in a manner in which it can be carefully accounted for and loaded into kits to ensure that it makes it into the helicopter tomorrow," says Mike. "Easier said than done. Obviously, forgetting just a small item or two would be a costly mistake for the project. Forgetting the dart gun insert or the drug would put an instant halt on the next day's capture, resulting in a costly trip back to base just to get the forgotten piece of equipment. The tattoo and ear punch equipment is essential for individually marking captured bears."

Aside from dealing with the equipment and the tools for capture, it is enormously important to quickly prep, fix, and store many of the biological samples to maximize sample quality and integrity. Blood left in the test tubes will deteriorate, so it is important to separate, or "spin down," the samples with heparin (a chemical that prevents blood from clotting in test tubes) to get serum as soon as possible and to put the blood in proper containers for long-term storage. Each sample of blood, fat, ear punch, and milk is stored in a specific container and frozen. Given the volume of samples that can come from successive days of capture, it is very easy to get backlogged and potentially compromise the sample catalog if the samples aren't fully dealt with on a daily basis.

Putting things in vials and bags and then labeling them takes a lot of time, too. A freezer in the field lab is used to temporarily store frozen samples before they are shipped out to labs in Anchorage or other destinations. New sampling, for instance, by the scientists at the University of Wyoming involves more specific physiological sampling of such things as muscle, breath, and blood.

When Kristin and Mike move their operation to the next two project bases, in Kaktovik and then Deadhorse, all of their lab equipment will be carefully packed in large plastic boxes called action packers. Each location has a room for a lab setup like the one at NARL in Barrow. There is a lot of equipment and sampling gear that is air-freighted to the new site, at considerable cost. This is the price of doing research in the Arctic. Typically, when transitioning to a new field station, one of the biologists accompanies the equipment and arrives before the capture crew. That person usually gets things set up pretty quickly so that any samples taken from captured bears during the flight over to the new base can be immediately processed and all the associated equipment cleaned and prepped as normal.

Tonight Kristin and Mike take turns entering data into the computer.

Mike downloads data from a GPS (a sophisticated airplane version of the ones we have in our cars) that contains all the information related to today's route—the exact search patterns that can help scientists analyze the capture and recapture work itself. The GPS records the daily flight path along with specific events, such as where and when bear tracks were followed, where there were seal kill sites, and where bears were encountered.

"We try to fly capture missions over as much of the regional area around our different field bases as possible," Mike says. "And should we find that bears are predominantly captured in some areas and absent from others, despite efforts to evenly distribute the capture effort, scientists will take a look at why this may be happening. Perhaps there are areas of much higher quality seal habitat that attract bears. Knowing what kind of search effort went into the study is therefore very important." All this data will be analyzed by the Polar Bear Research Project

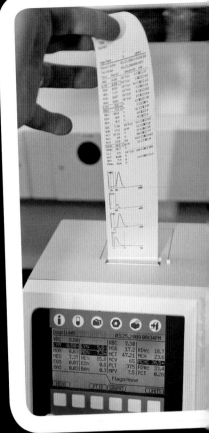

Some scientific tests of blood content require that the blood is analyzed as soon as possible. A small amount of blood from each bear is analyzed when the biologists return from the field. The sample tests show the relative health and chemical composition of the blood.

leader, George Durner, who studies the movement of bears in relationship to annual and long-term changes in sea ice conditions.

George explains, "We don't do this work just to handle cool animals. It's important to take the data we collect out there on the ice and turn it into useful information to address conservation questions. Thanks to the incredible efforts of Steve Amstrup and people at other agencies, we have a lot of data collected over a long period of time."

Polar bear studies in the southern Beaufort Sea expanded in 2009. The University of Wyoming provided a separate helicopter and crew and took additional biological samples to study the differences in polar bear stresses and body condition for those bears stranded on land during the summer months with those found on summer pack ice, now hundreds of

An Overview of Samples Taken in the Field and What They Are Used For

- Lip tattoo and ear tags: The purpose of these is to give each bear a unique identification number so that scientists know if it has been previously captured. This is part of the scientific protocol for estimating population size and vital rates (survival and reproduction).
- Measurements: skull size, length, axillary girth, and so on. These are for monitoring the size of bears in the population and can be used to assess responses of the population to environmental change (for example, poorer nutrition will result in smaller bears).
- Body mass index and body fat index scores: These are measurements that change with the seasons and food availability and give a good overall idea of a bear's actual physical condition. These measures are basic to an understanding of how bears may be coping with changes in their environment, such as increasing loss of winter pack ice.
- Body fat determined from bioelectrical impedance analysis (BIA): BIA is another measure of polar bear health in that it measures lipid (fatty acids) content.
- Fat biopsies: A small 6 mm punch is used to get a fat sample from the rump area of bears. Such samples can be used to examine bear exposure to environmental contaminants; fat samples also provide data on fatty acids, which are used to determine diet.

John Whiteman, a University of Wyoming graduate student, performs minor surgery on a polar bear to implant a small "data logger" just under its fat layer. The tiny data logger will record key information on body temperature changes over extended periods, giving scientists insight into potential environmental stresses placed on bears from seasonal weather changes. These data will be compared from bears that are forced to live onshore (because of retreating sea ice) versus bears that continue to use summer pack ice far out to sea.

Fat samples taken from polar bears in the field are put into cryo-freezer vials for permanent freezer storage. These samples can provide a great deal of important information, especially whether the bears have been exposed to a wide range of man-made chemical contaminants.

- Blood: Blood can be used for a variety of analyses, including contaminant assessments or to understand diet via levels of carbon and nitrogen stable isotopes, disease, and feeding physiology (e.g., ratios of urea to creatinine give an indication of whether a bear has fed recently or has been fasting). Blood can also be used for genetic studies (e.g., relatedness among individuals; difference in gene flow for different spatial regions of a population).
- Hair: Polar bear hair can be used to look at contaminants or diet via stable isotopes; hair can also be used for genetics studies.
- Pedal swabs: Scientists have collected these swabs from between the toes for researchers at the San Diego Zoo who are studying bear scent behavior, and nose swabs are collected for a variety of people looking at the presence of disease, particularly *Morbillivirus*.
- Other information: Scientists also take feces, milk (from lactating moms), and ear punch plugs (for genetic analyses). A vestigial premolar is taken from any previously uncaptured bear older than two years; the annual cementum rings can be used to determine the bear's age. Breeding conditions (estrus, testicles descended, etc.) are recorded. Tooth wear and breakage, scars, injuries, abnormalities, hair loss, or unusual features are also recorded.

Polar bear blood samples are pipetted into cryo-freezer vials for long-term storage.

A small punch is used to make a hole in the ear of each polar bear in order to attach a numbered plastic ear tag for individual identification. The skin and cartilage removed from the ear tag punch are kept in freezer vials and can be used for later genetic analyses.

When George Durner first came to
work on the Polar Bear Research Project, the management issues for polar
bears were all based on hunting; no one
was paying much attention to global
warming. It was all about the number
of polar bears people could shoot and
still maintain the population. "But at the
end of the 1990s," George says, "people
started noticing that there was not as
much ice in the summers as there used
to be. And then climate change issues
around polar bears took off, especially
in the last ten years."

George explains further: "That's
why telemetry is so important, and the
information we get from radio tracking.
We use sophisticated software to analyze data from spring captures and from
the collars." Basically, scientists are try-
ing to find out as much information as
they can on polar bear populations and
polar bear health.

George's interests focus on understanding the movement and distribution of bears as these factors relate
to sea ice and habitat, with a goal of
eventually determining how patterns of
habitat use affect population levels. He
says, "We're asking questions like: What
kind of sea ice is needed by polar bears?
In the eyes of a polar bear, not all sea
ice is equal. There are certain nuances,
and if you don't have enough of one

sort of ice or too much of another, this
can affect the distribution of bears."

Polar bears, George points out, seem
to prefer first-year ice (sea ice that has
not yet experienced summer melt),
where seals hang out most. They probably prefer ice that's relatively close to
open water but with sufficient ice and
pressure ridges around it that can provide refuge if weather conditions deteriorate. Throughout the Beaufort Sea,

bears prefer ice directly over the co
nental shelf because biologically th
where the waters are shallow and m
productive, the area that is likely to
support the greatest numbers of sea
The distribution of radio-tracked be
seems to show this pattern, too. In f
sea ice over the continental shelves
appears to be the most important
habitat for polar bears throughout t
Arctic Ocean. In addition to genera

The distribution of polar bear maternal dens in Alaska and neighboring regions. Data was collected by standardized VHF radio telemetry and satellite radio telemetry. This map is included because denning locations have been a major focus of polar bear research and this is a good example of how polar bear scientists use the data they collect. Source: Amstrup and Gardner 1994, Fischbach et al. 2007, Durner et al. 2010.

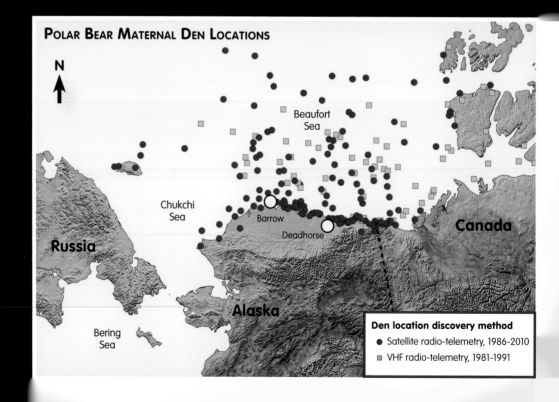

POLAR BEAR MATERNAL DEN LOCATIONS

N

Beaufort Sea

Chukchi Sea

Barrow

Deadhorse

Russia

Canada

Alaska

Bering Sea

Den location discovery method
● Satellite radio-telemetry, 1986-2010
■ VHF radio-telemetry, 1981-1991

The village of Barrow, in the distance to the left, is at the very top of Alaska, where the Chukchi and Beaufort seas converge. Strong currents and wind constantly change pack ice conditions, and huge leads of ocean water may open up dramatically, only to be slammed shut again as wind pushes enormous ice pans back together. Strong currents commonly make a large, open lead to the sea just north of Barrow, which has allowed the Iñupiaq people to harvest whales and other sea life for many centuries.

Eric Regehr of the U.S. Fish and Wildlife Service inspects a ringed seal just killed by a polar bear.

ing greater biological productivity than the deep waters, the shelf ice is usually more dynamic, causing the formation of leads and polynyas (persistent open water), areas of broken ice that provide a place where hunting seals can be more productive for polar bears.

George, who knows a lot about the relationship between the ice and the bears, maintains a positive outlook. "A lot of people may feel that we are at a tipping point," he says, "where we can't do anything about the melting ice and the downward direction that bear populations are headed. I guess my optimism comes from knowing that humans *can* make a difference. The scientific evidence shows a close relationship of greenhouse gases to climate change and therefore to declines in Arctic sea ice. This suggests that by reducing the amount of carbon dioxide and other greenhouse gases we pump into the air, humans may be able to stop further losses of Arctic sea ice and improve the chances for the survival of polar bears.

"It's not a hopeless situation by any means," he continues. "The scientific models indicate that reducing greenhouse gas emissions gives a more favorable outlook for polar bear populations.

Regardless, it's going to be a very difficult problem to address. No one person or one country can do it on its own. It will take efforts by humans across the whole world to recognize that we can make a difference and avert a bad problem."

Not only does George Durner crunch numbers from the satellite tracking data from the radio collars on female bears, but he also depends on all the flight data information entered daily into the project field computer during

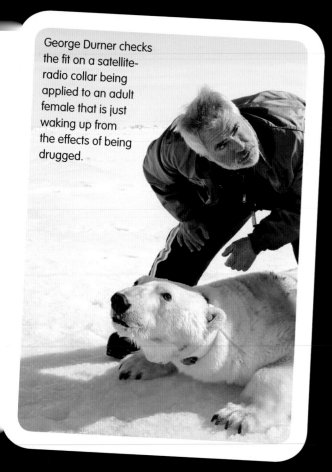

George Durner checks the fit on a satellite-radio collar being applied to an adult female that is just waking up from the effects of being drugged.

George Durner holds a hand-captured cub of the year after it is anesthetized.

…g captures. That's what Kristin is
…ng now, copying into the comput-
…he information she recorded ear-
…on the two bears. The USGS Polar
…Research Project uses a wonderful
…puter program that progressively
…ws the steps of the flight day, and
…n Kristin gets to the time when the
…ure occurred, another window on

the screen opens to record all the capture data.

Data entry is crucial and very time-
consuming. After the flight data, all
the data from the bear capture sheet is
entered, too. Those data are ultimately
entered into a huge population database so that age and sex, bear condition
and growth, breeding status, productiv-

…ty, and so on can be analyzed late…
George, Steve, and others. This we…
of information helps scientists gaug…
the overall population stability and…
changes over time.

It's midnight when Ryan, Kristin…
Mike close the door to the lab and …
to their bunks for a few hours of sl…
before they'll do this all again.

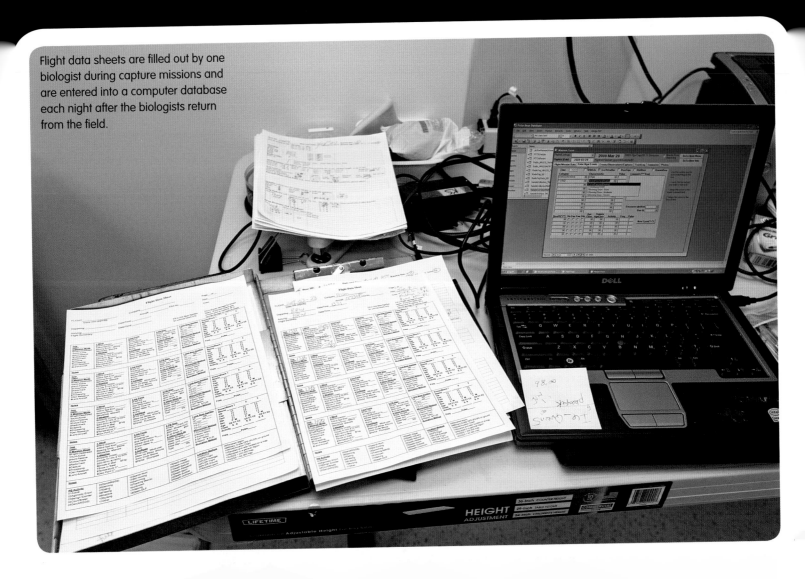

Flight data sheets are filled out by one biologist during capture missions and are entered into a computer database each night after the biologists return from the field.

A female bear with one of her yearling cubs at a whale bone pile. Whales harvested by the Iñupiat provide a food source for bears that are stranded on land when the sea ice pack retreats north. What would happen to the bears in those years when few or no whales are harvested?

Searching the Bone Pile

The USGS has determined that a satellite transmitter collar has been shed, or perhaps the bear wearing the collar is dead. Those are the only possible explanations when the satellite location for that radio doesn't move at all for a period of several days. Collars are expensive; this one is still active and can be reused.

Today's weather does not look promising for captures, but the first thing the team needs to do is locate this lost collar buried somewhere near the bone pile just north of Barrow, where the Iñupiat put the carcasses of the bowhead whales after they harvest them during the fall whaling season. Polar bears come to the massive pile of bones to feed throughout the year, and some people believe it's the pile itself that actually increases the number of bears that find their way to town looking for a meal. A number of years ago, no fewer than ninety bears wandered through the streets of Barrow and the surrounding area.

Mike has had considerable experience retrieving lost collars in other wildlife research projects and has been out maybe half a dozen times during his years in the Arctic to retrieve shed polar bear collars. Of course it's expensive to go find a distant collar, with the

Two yearling males roughhouse on the beach. This photo was taken in fall near a whale bone pile where bears come to feed.

The VHF radio receiver indicates that a shed polar bear collar is somewhere just underfoot and requires some tough digging in the ice and snow pack to find.

cost of fuel and time, but it's equally if not more important to find a collar in order to determine whether a bear has died or has just dropped it.

At the airport, Gaylen says, "Man, it's windy" as he runs through his inspection of N73LF. "Minus thirty, but feels a lot worse with the wind," he calls as Kristin and Mike and Joe pack the last of the capture gear. Today is supposed to be a regular capture run, but it's iffy. It's more difficult and dangerous to make a darting run in winds over thirty miles an hour, and it's more stressful on bears, especially small cubs, to drug them in conditions of low temperatures and high winds.

As the helo lifts off the runway, Joe says, "Flight service says it's going to drop down to forty-two below."

Kristin counters, "We're not going to do much today, just find the collar probably."

Joe optimistically calls to Gaylen on the radio, "We'll be back at seven." The wind is gusting to twenty-two miles per hour.

Mike advises Joe to go up a few thousand feet to get a good signal from the lost collar. The higher you are, the farther the collar transmisson beeps can be heard. "What you want to do," says Mike, "is locate the distant signal at altitude, then continually drop down,

and by moving the helo in progressively smaller box patterns, we can direct the helo very close to the collar on the ground."

Mike notices that the lead has opened up even more than yesterday. "Holy smoke, there's lots of water," he says. It's more water than Mike can remember this early in the season.

Joe takes the helo over the bone pile and hovers, facing in different directions as Kristin homes in on the shed

collar. She also gives the known satellite coordinates of the place the collar has been transmitting from. Each collar has a unique frequency, and now Kristin is focusing on that one.

"Might be in the water," Joe suggests.

Mike says, "No. We wouldn't get a signal if it was in the water. You can get a signal if it's under some ice a little ways, though. We picked up a signal from a stationary collar last year that was under ice right at the edge of a

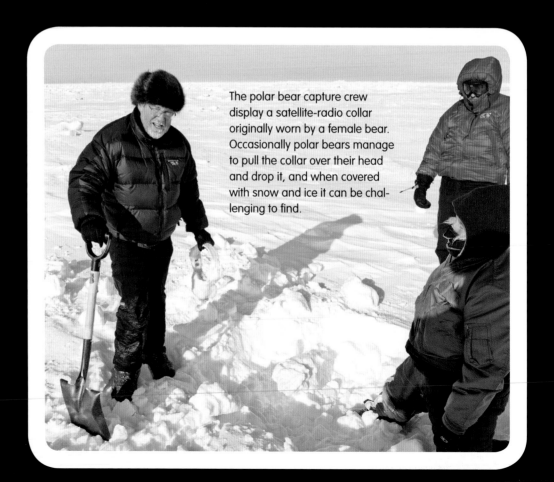

The polar bear capture crew display a satellite-radio collar originally worn by a female bear. Occasionally polar bears manage to pull the collar over their head and drop it, and when covered with snow and ice it can be challenging to find.

ead, but we couldn't dig down enough to get to it without risking breaking into the lead. As we dug, water came up through the hole."

Kristin is getting a strong signal, and Joe puts the helo down so that Mike and Kristin can walk with the VHF receiver in their hands, their backs to the fierce wind.

As Kristin and Mike press forward with shovel and receiver, Mike switches to a short coax antenna lead to the receiver to get a better signal and further narrow the site. They are walking in grid patterns over a small patch of snow and ice. And finally, they get within inches of the invisible collar. This one is not on the surface, so they have to dig, fighting the harsh wind that is now dropping the temperature closer to fifty below.

The snow blows across the ice like a sandstorm in the desert. There's bear poop everywhere. Mike and Kristin abandon the receiver to hack at the frozen snow with a pick and shovel. The loose snow is flying in the wind like horsehair.

Then Mike pulls it out of the snow. Everyone smiles. It's an Arctic treasure scene. It's amazing that they can find this little white ring in all that snow and whipping wind. The great thing is that the collar is not attached to a dead

bear; it was simply shed.

When they return to the helo, Kristin and Mike decide that these are not good conditions for bear capture. But as they fly low and slow back to Barrow, everyone sees that there are tracks close to town, tracks that were not there on the way out. That's how quickly things can change during polar bear capture work. There is no such thing as a typical day.

As the crew grabs all the gear out of the helicopter in Barrow—today's unused darts and the dart gun and the tools for marking, measuring, and collecting biological samples—someone asks Kristin if she'll take a vacation after the capture season. Quickly she says, "Yeah," but then thinks again. "Well, who wants to leave Alaska in the summer?"

After she and Mike work in Barrow for a few more weeks, they will move the capture operation to Kaktovik and Deadhorse, and it'll be early May. At this time of year in the Arctic, it's almost impossible to imagine

Before each capture mission, the helicopter mechanic and pilot perform important safety checks while biologists load equipment into storage compartments.

the month of May as most of us think of it. Impossible to imagine that spring could ever come to Alaska when it's this windy, this cold, this snowy, this white, here in a perfect Arctic icescape where the polar bear reigns supreme—a land of seals, Iñupiaq whale hunters, and the impending coming of the whales.

How could we ever lose or jeopardize this polar bear paradise? And most of all, what can we do to make sure it doesn't disappear forever?

A Final Conversation with Dr. Steven Amstrup About Climate Change and the Future of Polar Bears

Steve Amstrup speaks bluntly about the future. "Today the single biggest threat to polar bears is the decline in their habitat that's likely to occur because of global warming. Some people might say they don't believe in global warming, or that humans don't have the ability to influence the climate. But the fundamental laws of physics show that if more heat-trapping (greenhouse) gases like carbon dioxide—which come from burning fossil fuels—are put into the atmosphere, the earth will be a warmer place."

That doesn't mean, Steve says, that there won't be natural fluctuations in temperature. "Last summer Alaska was unusually cool, and some people asked, 'So what happened to global warming?' But they're responding to fluctuations in *weather,* not *climate.*" It was a cold and wet summer because of natural weather oscillations, but even so, it was warmer than it would have been had we had lower concentrations of greenhouse gases.

So what does all this mean for the polar bear's future?

A warmer world translates into less sea ice. Although there is uncertainty about near-term changes, climate scientists overwhelmingly agree that over the next few decades, physical laws will guarantee substantial earth warming. Natural fluctuations prevent knowing exactly when the first ice-free summer will occur in the Arctic—something polar bear scientists are really concerned about for the bears—but if greenhouse gas concentrations continue to grow, ice-free summers are guaranteed.

Climate models indicate that sea ice will return in winter for some time to come, even as summer absences become longer.

Steve Amstrup with a large male polar bear.

How prolonged an ice-free season polar bears can survive, however, is something we need to understand, we already know from southerly portions of the polar bear range that an absence of sea ice for prolonged summer periods in the Arctic will have a serious impact on bears.

"George Durner's work has shown us that polar bears prefer to hunt on ice over shallow water," Steve says. In the polar basin north of Alaska, the shallow water areas lie over what is known as the continental shelf and stretch several hundred miles offshore to the north. These continental shelf waters are the most biologically productive areas of the southern Beaufort Sea, and they support an enormous abundance and diversity of fish and other sea life, which in turn supports greater numbers of seals and hence greater numbers of polar bears.

To study polar bears that are on sea ice far from land, scientists worked with the U.S. Coast Guard. The scientists spent five weeks living on this ship, the *Polar Sea,* which is specially designed to break through sea ice. Helicopters were flown from the ship to capture and study polar bears.

"As a result of global warming today, the summer sea ice pack now retreats much farther north and well away from the continental shelf. So bears that remain on the summer sea ice, as most of the population does, find themselves hundreds of miles north of the continental shelf and over very deep water that is much less productive for fish, seals, and polar bears. We have hypothesized," Steve says, "that those bears might not be doing so well out there. In the summertime, seals may not be following the ice to the far north reaches. What, then, are those bears on the distant pack ice doing for food?"

It is hoped that studies begun in 2010 will help scientists assess how bears are faring on the distant pack ice. George Durner and other scientists took an icebreaker—a ship designed to break a channel through ice—into the retreating sea ice for a first-ever look at what's happening. "We're hopeful that we can catch bears, monitor their condition, and determine whether they're doing better or worse than the bears that are stuck on land in the summertime."

Steve says that the other side of the coin is an increasing number of bears in northern Alaska getting stuck on land when the sea ice retreats. "There is very little natural food on the north shore of Alaska that will substitute for the nutrition that bears get from hunting seals on sea ice. On land in northern Alaska, polar bears are taking advan-

A large male is being moved by helicopter away from a pressure ridge for processing.

tage of the carcasses from bowhead whales traditionally taken by Iñupiaq Eskimos for subsistence purposes. These whale carcasses are a nutrition source that is artificial from the standpoint of polar bear evolutionary history. But the bears are not averse to taking advantage of bowhead whale carcasses or any other available food source when they're stuck on land and hungry." A potential problem with this artificial feeding is that it can unnaturally concentrate bears, sometimes near humans, resulting in increased risks for both bears and people.

Scientists know that polar bears have survived warm periods in the past. The genetic record suggests that polar bears have been around for some 200,000 to 300,000 years, maybe longer. Geneticists are still sorting out just how long ago polar bears first separated from their brown bear ancestors, but if they have been around for a quarter of a million years, they have gone through two periods that were actually warmer than now—the last interglacial period of around 120,000 years ago and the Holocene thermal maximum of around 10,000 years ago.

"A difference between those warmings of 120,000 and 10,000 years ago and now," says Steve, "is that we didn't have nearly as many humans out there competing with bears and otherwise affecting their security. Unless we do something about greenhouse gas emissions, it will be warmer by the middle to the latter part of this century than it has been at any time during the evolutionary history of polar bears. And as temperatures rise and habitat is reduced, polar bears are going to be competing with a lot of human uses of their environment."

Steve pauses, choosing his words carefully. When he begins again, his voice is strong and clear. "Everyone who is concerned about polar bears must realize that individual greenhouse gas footprints will affect the polar bear's future. As a message to future generations, I'd say the most important thing is to come to grips with the idea that we humans are responsible for the rapid acceleration of global climate change. Individually and as societies we must do everything we can to mitigate or minimize our own greenhouse gas contributions. That is the only real hope of reversing the inevitable losses of polar bear habitat."

GLOSSARY

bearded seal: a large Arctic seal with a tuft of long whiskers on each side of its muzzle. Adults run 7 to 9 feet and 600 to 750 pounds. The bearded seal is a major food source for the polar bear, and the skin is used by Iñupiaq Eskimos in Alaska to cover their traditional whaling boats, called *umiaqs*.

Bioelectrical impedance analysis (BIA): a commonly used method for estimating body composition. BIA actually determines the electrical impedance, or opposition to the flow of an electric current through body tissues, which can then be used to calculate an estimate of total body water (TBW). TBW can be used to estimate fat-free body mass and, by comparison with body weight, body fat.

bowhead whale: a black whale that lives in the Arctic seas and feeds by using its baleen to skim plankton and krill near the surface of the water.

capture and recapture: a method of estimating populations of wildlife that cannot be reasonably counted.

carbon dioxide (CO²): a colorless, odorless gas produced by burning fuels and by the decay and respiration of vegetation. It is a powerful greenhouse gas and is removed from the air by plants in photosynthesis.

climate: average weather conditions (temperature, precipitation, winds) over years for a particular region and time period.

continental shelf: area of seabed around a large landmass, where the sea is relatively shallow compared with the open ocean.

first-year ice: sea ice of not more than one winter's growth.

fossil fuels: natural fuels such as coal, gas, and oil, which were formed from the remains of plankton and vegetation over millions of years.

global warming: a rise in the overall temperature of the earth's atmosphere that threatens the environment and is caused by increased levels of greenhouse gases such as carbon dioxide.

greenhouse effect: the trapping of the earth's heat in the lower atmosphere by greenhouse gases. At a low level, this effect keeps the earth warm enough to support life and does not threaten the environment.

greenhouse gas: gas that slows the escape of heat from the earth into space. Most greenhouse gases, such as carbon dioxide, ozone, methane, and nitrous oxide, are pollutants.

Ordinary water vapor is also a powerful greenhouse gas.

habitat: the natural home or environment of an animal, plant, or other organism. Includes the food source.

Sometimes big males refuse to run from a helicopter.

A mother polar bear travels with two yearlings.

International Union for Conservation of Nature (IUCN): the world's main authority on the conservation status of species. A series of Regional Red Lists, produced by countries or organizations, assess the risk of extinction of species within a political management unit.

Iñupiaq Eskimo (plural **Iñupiat**): a member of an indigenous group of Eskimos living in northern and northwestern Alaska.

IUCN Red List of Threatened Species (also known as the IUCN Red List or Red Data List): the world's most comprehensive inventory of the global conservation status of plant and animal species.

open lead: a linear section of open water between the shorefast ice and the pack ice.

pack ice: a term used in a wide sense to include any area of sea ice other than shorefast ice.

polar ice pack: large areas of pack ice formed from seawater in the earth's polar regions, known as polar ice caps: the Arctic ice pack (or Arctic ice cap) of the Arctic Ocean and the Antarctic ice pack of the Southern Ocean, that fringes the Antarctic ice sheet. Polar ice packs significantly change in size as a result of seasonal changes during the year.

pressure ridge: a ridge of ice, up to 100 feet (30 meters) high and sometimes several kilometers long, produced from the shear forces of moving sea ice.

ringed seal: the most common and smallest seal species in the Arctic. They get their name from the light-colored circular patterns that appear on their darker gray backs.

sea ice: any form of ice found at sea that has originated from the freezing of seawater. It presents the main kind of ice encountered at sea.

shorefast ice: ice that is attached to the shore but can break free; the ice shelf that extends from the land. This ice may be formed in place from seawater or by the freezing in place of floating ice that comes to shore.

Polar bears walk gingerly over thin ice to try to keep from breaking through.

POLAR BEAR FIELD GUIDE

Polar Bear (*Ursus maritimus*)

- Polar bears are found mostly within the Arctic Circle in areas where sea ice allows them to catch enough food to survive any period of ice absence.

- It is estimated that some 20,000 to 25,000 polar bears are living in the world today.

- The polar bears' range includes areas within the borders of five "circumpolar" nations: United States (Alaska), Canada, Denmark (Greenland), Norway (Svalbard), and Russia.

- Polar bears are mostly solitary animals except when they are mating, when a mother has cubs, or when they are concentrating on land at large food sources.

- Polar bears are the largest land carnivore and largest bear (the Kodiak bear is close in size).

- Adult male polar bears weigh 770 to 1,500 pounds (350–680 kg); adult females are about half that size.

- The largest polar bear on record was a male from Kotzebue Sound in northwestern Alaska in 1960: he weighed 2,210 pounds (1,002 kg).

- Adult male polar bears typically live into their late teens and early twenties; adult females live into their late twenties and sometimes even early thirties.

- Polar bears evolved from the brown bear thousands of years ago; the most recent estimate, made from a jawbone found on Svalbard, suggests that they have been around for at least 150,000 years.

- The primary food source for polar bears is the ringed seal, but they also hunt bearded seals, walrus, and beluga whales and will scavenge beached whales and walrus and seal carcasses found along the coast.

- The polar bear is a stealth hunter; seal victims are often unaware of bears in the area until they are attacked.

- Polar bears are especially adapted to the polar marine environment as they depend on the sea ice to successfully hunt seals.

- The particular physical adaptations of polar bears include a camouflage-white coloration of the fur; dense underfur with an outer layer of water-repellent hairs; large "furred" feet to distribute weight on snow and thin ice and aid in swimming; small, soft bumps on the soles of their feet that provide traction on slippery ice; short, sharp, stocky nonretractable claws for gripping ice and prey; and the ability to store large amounts of fat for use when food is unavailable.

- Polar bears are excellent swimmers; they can swim more than 200 miles (320 km) in open water under calm conditions. Their body fat provides buoyancy, and they use only their front paws for paddling. They can swim at 6 miles per hour (9.7 kmh).

- A polar bear's average walking speed is 3.5 miles per hour (5.6 kmh) in a lumbering gait, but it can sprint up to 25 miles per hour (40 kmh).

- Polar bears have an extraordinary sense of smell. They can detect prey from well over 20 miles (32 km) away.

- Although often stereotyped as very aggressive, polar bears are typically cautious and often choose to escape rather than fight. Attacks on humans are very rare.

- Polar bears molt their fur from May to August but do not shed white hairs for a darker color, as most Arctic animals do in order to be camouflaged in summer. Polar bears stay white in order to hunt on sea ice.

- Female polar bears usually breed once every three years, during April and May.

- When the mother gives birth, it is generally to one or two cubs in December and January (three cubs is relatively rare). The cubs weigh 16 to 24 ounces (.5–.7 kg) and remain with their mother for about 2.25 years.

- In Hudson Bay, James Bay, and other areas, the sea ice melts entirely on an annual cycle, forcing bears to wait and fast on land until the next freeze-up.

- In summer, in the Chukchi and Beaufort seas, most polar bears follow the pack ice north as the year-round ice retreats farther from land; others stay on land to wait for the ice to return or to scavenge at food sources made available by humans.

- Generally, seals migrate to follow sea ice flow; in turn, polar bears follow their prey.

- The IUCN (International Union for Conservation of Nature) now lists global warming as the most significant threat to polar bears because the rapid melt and decline of sea ice habitat reduces the polar bear's ability to find sufficient food.

SUGGESTED BOOKS

FOR YOUNGER READERS:

DeBeer, Hans. *Little Polar Bear* (fiction). New York: North-South Books, 1987.

George, Jean Craighead. *The Last Polar Bear*, illustrated by Wendell Minor. New York: HarperCollins, 2009.

Hirsch, Rebecca E. *Top 50 Reasons to Care About Polar Bears: Animals in Peril*. Berkeley Heights, N.J.: Enslow Publishers, 2010.

Ovsyanikov, Nikita. *Polar Bears* (Worldlife Library). Minneapolis: Voyageur Press, 1998.

Rosing, Norbert. *The World of the Polar Bear*. Buffalo, N.Y.: Firefly Books, 2010.

Rosing, Norbert, and Elizabeth Carney. *Face to Face with Polar Bears*. Des Moines: National Geographic Children's Books, 2009.

Stirling, Ian. *Bears*. San Francisco: Sierra Club Books for Children, 1992.

FOR OLDER READERS:

Ellis, Richard. *On Thin Ice: The Changing World of the Polar Bear*. New York: Knopf, 2009.

Mulvaney, Kieran. *The Great White Bear: A Natural and Unnatural History of the Polar Bear*. Boston: Houghton Mifflin Harcourt, 2011.

Stirling, Ian. *Polar Bears*. Ann Arbor: University of Michigan Press, 1999.

POLAR BEAR WEBSITES

Polar Bears International

www.polarbearsinternational.org
Polar Bears International is a nonprofit organization dedicated to the worldwide conservation of the polar bear and its habitat through research, stewardship, and education. PBI provides scientific resources and information on polar bears and their habitat to institutions and the general public worldwide.

Sign up for Polar Bears International's e-newsletter:
www.polarbearsinternational.org/enews

Status report on polar bears:
www.polarbearsinternational.org/polar-bears/will-polar-bears-survive

Questions about polar bears:
www.polarbearsinternational.org/polar-bears/faq

Short videos of polar bear experts:
www.polarbearsinternational.org/polar-bears/what-the-experts-say

Climate change and polar bears:
www.polarbearsinternational.org/polar-bears/climate-change

The World Wildlife Fund

The World Wildlife Fund supports field research by the world's foremost experts on polar bears to find out how climate change will affect their long-term condition. Polar Bear conservation at the World Wildlife Fund:
www.worldwildlife.org/species/finder/polar-bear/polarbear.html
A great list of polar bear publications from the World Wildlife Fund:
www.worldwildlife.org/species/finder/polar-bear/publications.html

Panda.Org

www.panda.org/Arctic
Panda.Org helps young readers understand this fascinating part of the globe.

In Alaska

USGS Alaska polar bear research:
alaska.usgs.gov/science/biology/polar_bears/index.html
Fish and Wildlife Service, Alaska region:
alaska.fws.gov
alaska.fws.gov/fisheries/mmm/polarbear/facts.htm

The Polar Bear Specialist Group (PBSG) of the IUCN Species Survival Commission

pbsg.npolar.no/en/index.html
The PBSG is the authoritative source for information on the world's polar bears—one of IUCN/SSC's more than one hundred specialist groups that work to produce and compile scientific knowledge about the species and give independent scientific advice to decision makers and management authorities.

The International Association for Bear Research and Management, IUCN/SSC Bear Specialist Group

www.bearbiology.com
The goal of the International Association for Bear Research and Management (IBA) is to promote the conservation and restoration of the world's bears through science-based research, management, and education.

National Snow and Ice Data Center (NSIDC), Arctic Sea ice news

nsidc.org/about/expertise/overview.html
NSIDC supports research into our world's frozen realms: the snow, ice, glaciers, frozen

ground, and climate interactions that make up the earth's cryosphere.

Arctic photography

For more great polar bear photos, visit Daniel J. Cox's website:

www.naturalexposures.com

QUOTED SOURCES

Tape-Recorded Interviews

Steve Amstrup, George Durner, and Kristin Simac (USGS Polar Bear Research Project), Mike Lockhart (Polar Bears International), Geoff York (World Wildlife Fund), Karyn Rode (U.S. Fish and Wildlife Service), Eugene Brower (Barrow Whaling Captains Association), Craig George (Wildlife Management, North Slope Borough, Barrow, Alaska), and Joe Fieldman and Gaylen Jensen (Prism Helicopters).

Books

Ellis, Richard. *On Thin Ice: The Changing World of the Polar Bear*. New York: Knopf, 2009.

Kazlowski, Steven. *The Last Polar Bear: Facing the Truth of a Warming World*. Seattle: Braided River, An Imprint of Mountaineers Books, 2008.

Rosing, Norbert. *The World of the Polar Bear*. Buffalo, N.Y.: Firefly Books, 2010.

Rosing, Norbert, and Elizabeth Carney. *Face to Face with Polar Bears*. Des Moines: National Geographic Children's Books, 2009.

Stirling, Ian. *Polar Bears*. Ann Arbor: University of Michigan Press, 1999.

Articles and Chapters

Amstrup, S. C. "Polar bear, Ursus maritimus." pp. 587–610 in G. A. Feldhamer, B. C. Thompson, and J. A. Chapman (eds.). *Wild Mammals of North America: Biology, Management, and Conservation*. Baltimore: Johns Hopkins University Press, 2003.

Lockhart, Mike. "A Day in the Life of a Field Biologist." *Polar Bears International Newsletter*, May 8, 2009.

Polar Bears International newsletters 2005–9.

Revkin, Andy (environmental journalist). *New York Times* articles 2005–10.

Rode, Karyn, and George Durner. "Polar Bear Research in the Chukchi Sea: A Synopsis of 2008 Field Work." U.S. Fish and Wildlife Service.

"Your Climate, Your Future: An Interdisciplinary Approach to Incorporating Climate Change in your Classroom." PDF file: worldwildlife.org/climate/curriculum/WWFBinaryitem5977.pdf

Websites

Polar Bears International: polarbearsinternational.org

Polar Bear Conservation at the World Wildlife Fund: worldwildlife.org/species/finder/polarbear/polarbear.html

USGS Alaska polar bear research: alaska.usgs.gov/science/biology/polar_bears/index.html

Fish and Wildlife Service, Alaska Region: alaska.fws.gov/fisheries/mmm/polarbear/facts.htm

PHOTO CREDITS

Photos by Mike Lockhart except the following:

Author: 5 (bottom), 16, 17, 19 (top & bottom), 23 (center & right), 24 (both), 27 (both), 29 (both), 32 (bottom), 34 (right), 35 (insert), 37 (bottom), 41, 42 (center & top), 43 (both), 44 (center & left), 45, 46 (right), 51, 52 (both), 53, 56, 57, 58, 59 (both), 60, 61 (right), 62 (right), 63 (both), 65 (top), 67, 69 (right), 70 (right), 71.

Siede Preis/Photodisc/Getty Images: (background) 2, 14, 15, 25, 41, 48, 49, 72, 73, 76, 77, 80.

John Whiteman: 8, 39 (right), 73.

Geoff York: 13.

Steve Amstrup: 22 (left).

Don Farrall/Photodisc/Getty Images: (background) 56, 57, 62, 63, 74, 75.

A mother bear watches a passing helicopter while nursing her new cub.

INDEX

Page numbers in bold type refer to photographs and their captions.